Department of
the Treasury

Office of Federal Housing
Enterprise Oversight

Securities and Exchange
Commission

STAFF REPORT:
ENHANCING DISCLOSURE IN THE MORTGAGE-BACKED SECURITIES MARKETS

A Staff Report of the Task Force on Mortgage-Backed Securities Disclosure

January 2003

Staff Report:
Enhancing Disclosure in the Mortgage-Backed Securities Markets

A Staff Report of the Task Force on Mortgage-Backed Securities Disclosure

Contents

Executive Summary	1
I. Introduction	4
II. Background	5
A. Issuers	5
B. MBS Investors	6
C. Mortgage-Backed Securities	7
1. Secondary Mortgage Market Enhancement Act of 1984	8
2. Effect of Tax Laws on MBS Markets	8
3. Types of Underlying Mortgage Loans	9
4. Guarantees or Credit Enhancements	11
5. Risks – Prepayment and Credit	11
a. Prepayment Risk	11
b. Credit Risk	12
D. Structure of the MBS	13
1. Pass-Through Securities	13
2. REMICS	14
E. Creation and Sales of GSE and Ginnie Mae MBS	15
1. Creation of GSE and Ginnie Mae MBS	15
2. The To-Be-Announced Market	16
3. Types of Trades of TBA-Eligible MBS	20
4. Dollar Rolls	21
F. Creation and Sales of Private-label MBS	22
1. Creation of Private-label MBS	22
2. Sales of Private-label MBS	23
G. Statutes Governing the Offer and Sale of MBS	23
III. Current Disclosure Practices	26
A. General	26
B. Offering Documents	26
1. Private-label Offering Materials	26
2. GSE and Ginnie Mae Offering Materials	28
C. Post-Offering Disclosures	28
1. Private-label MBS	28
2. GSE and Ginnie Mae MBS	29
D. Particular Issues Addressed by Disclosure	29
1. Prepayment Risk	30
2. Credit Risk	30
E. Types of Disclosures	31

	1. Loan Terms		31
		a. Coupon or Interest Rates on Underlying Loans	31
		b. Loan Maturity Dates and Loan Age	32
		c. Loan Size	34
		d. Points Paid at Settlement	34
	2. Property Information		34
		a. Geographic Distribution	35
		b. Property Types	35
		c. Occupancy Types	35
		d. Loan-to-Value Ratio	36
	3. Borrower Information		37
		a. Credit Scores	37
		b. Loan Documentation	37
		c. Loan Purpose	38
		d. Borrower Debt-to-Income Ratios	38
	4. Sellers, Originators and Servicers		38
		a. Seller Identification	38
		b. Servicer Identification	39
IV. Information Imbalance Issues			40
V. Findings			43
Appendix A			A-1
Appendix B			B-1

EXECUTIVE SUMMARY

Staff of the Department of the Treasury ("Treasury"), the Office of Federal Housing Enterprise Oversight ("OFHEO"), and the Securities and Exchange Commission (the "Commission") formed a joint task force ("Task Force") in August 2002 to conduct a study of disclosures in offerings of mortgage-backed securities ("MBS"). The purpose of the joint study was to evaluate current disclosure practices and consider whether disclosure enhancements are desirable in assisting investors to make informed investment decisions.

In conducting the study, the Task Force reviewed the history and development of the MBS markets, the current disclosure requirements for these securities, and market-driven industry disclosure practices and standards. The Task Force also interviewed a variety of MBS issuers and investors, and other experienced market participants and observers, which provided the Task Force with additional perspectives about the evolution of the MBS markets, including changing disclosure standards. The Task Force received recommendations concerning changes to current disclosure standards based on investor needs, and assessments as to the likely impact of additional disclosure on the MBS markets' continued smooth functioning and liquidity. This report contains the Task Force's findings, conclusions, and recommendations regarding enhanced MBS disclosures.

Government sponsored enterprises ("GSEs") – the Federal National Mortgage Association ("Fannie Mae") and the Federal Home Loan Mortgage Corporation ("Freddie Mac") – as well as a wholly-owned federal government corporation – the Government National Mortgage Association ("Ginnie Mae") – played a major role in creating the MBS markets and today remain the largest issuers. Privately owned financial institutions have become increasingly important as issuers in the so-called "private-label" market. The MBS markets are estimated to have grown by more than 800% in the past two decades. During this time, the structure of MBS vehicles or products – whether issued by the GSEs, by Ginnie Mae, or by private-label issuers – has evolved and become significantly more complex. MBS investors continue to be almost exclusively institutional, but their expressed needs have changed with the evolving market and economic conditions. In recent years, investors have focused much more time, attention and resources on the evaluation of prepayment risk and, in the case of private label MBS, credit risk.

The Task Force found that the significant degree of evolution in disclosure standards in the offer and sale of MBS – whether of GSEs, Ginnie Mae or private-label MBS – in the past has been nearly entirely market driven. Market participants interviewed by the Task Force indicate that the changes have been considered beneficial to the market.

In interviews with the Task Force, MBS market participants also agreed, almost without exception, that the significant changes in disclosure did not affect the highly liquid nature of the GSE and Ginnie Mae pass-through and to-be-announced markets, and MBS markets generally operate reliably and efficiently. Yet, the Task Force also found that most market participants with whom it spoke, as well as most lenders and non-GSE issuers, believe the MBS markets could function better with additional pool-level disclosure. Moreover, consistent with their past experiences with changes in disclosure, these market participants expressed confidence that additional pool-level disclosures would not have a significant adverse effect on the markets' liquidity.

Based on the study, the Task Force has concluded that additional pool-level disclosures would be both useful and feasible. Market participants interviewed by the Task Force were clear in suggesting additional information that they believed would be useful. This report sets forth and describes the most frequently mentioned information that market participants recommended be disclosed to supplement currently disclosed information. Examples of additional disclosure items that market participants suggested would present few practical obstacles are:

- loan purpose;
- original loan-to-value ratios;
- standardized credit scores of borrowers;
- servicer information;
- occupancy status; and
- property type.

The Task Force believes there are no significant obstacles to the introduction of these additional pool-level disclosures and that the benefits of enhanced transparency would ultimately outweigh any costs. To implement additional disclosures, the Task Force recommends that investor interest and issues of practicality should be key criteria used to determine the specific items for additional disclosure in the MBS markets, as well as the appropriate timing and method of providing this additional disclosure. In the past, industry groups and other market participants have stepped forward to coordinate and implement additional disclosures in the MBS market. The Task Force encourages a continuation of this approach at this time. If market forces are unable to reach consensus on disclosure enhancements, the agencies represented on the Task Force will need to consider what additional action might be appropriate.

In addition to its review of MBS disclosures, the Task Force inquired about allegations of selective MBS selling and purchasing practices arising from possible information imbalances among market participants. The Task Force looked at policies and procedures regarding information barriers at the GSEs. In addition, OFHEO reviewed OFHEO examination reports and inquiries of the GSEs as to specific allegations. Though questioned by the Task Force about such allegations, interviewees provided no evidence to substantiate allegations of improper activity.

The Treasury, the Commission, and OFHEO will, in their separate capacities, continue to monitor the MBS markets to assess the implementation and potential impact of enhanced MBS disclosures. If future developments warrant, the Task Force members, in their separate capacities or jointly as they agree appropriate, could consider what additional steps might help provide additional, useful disclosures to MBS investors and market participants.

I. INTRODUCTION

In July of 2002, Treasury, OFHEO and the Commission made a joint announcement regarding the intention of Fannie Mae and Freddie Mac to voluntarily register their common stock under the Securities Exchange Act of 1934 (the "Exchange Act"). This voluntary registration, when in place, will trigger periodic disclosures regarding the GSEs. Treasury, OFHEO and the Commission also indicated they would review disclosure requirements and practices in the MBS markets, which would not be affected under this voluntary registration initiative. The purpose of the review on primary offering disclosures for MBS, which culminated in this report, was to examine disclosures to all investors in these securities, with a view to enhancing the availability of information that investors should have to evaluate the securities in the MBS markets and make investment decisions.

Staff from Treasury, OFHEO and the Commission, acting as the Task Force, have conducted the review of the disclosure practices in the MBS markets.[1] The Task Force focused on disclosures currently provided by all types of MBS issuers and considered whether disclosure improvements were desirable in assisting investors to evaluate securities in the MBS markets and make informed investment decisions.

The Task Force reviewed regulatory disclosure requirements and current industry disclosure practices. The Task Force also interviewed Fannie Mae, Freddie Mac and Ginnie Mae, private-label issuers, institutional investors, dealers, individual analysts, MBS market and real estate finance trade groups, pension funds and others involved in the markets to hear their views ranging from evaluations of current markets, how the markets function and particular concerns regarding disclosures.[2]

As background to the Task Force's findings, the report discusses the development and operation of the MBS markets, the various market participants, and the types of MBS sold. The report also addresses current disclosure practices and investor interest regarding the assets of and structures used for the securitization vehicles, credit and repayment sources and other risks affecting the repayment and value of the MBS, and information imbalance issues. Finally, the report notes categories of information that the Task Force believes would enhance disclosures in the MBS markets.

---

[1] The Task Force consisted of personnel from the Department of Treasury's Office of the Under Secretary for Domestic Finance and the Office of General Counsel, from OFHEO's Office of General Counsel, Office of Policy Analysis and Research and the Office of the Director and from the Commission's Division of Corporation Finance.

[2] Appendix A lists the market participants who were interviewed.

II. BACKGROUND

The Task Force considered current MBS disclosures in the context of the market's origins and growth, the market's participants – including issuers, investors and others – the structure and risks of MBS, and the current laws governing the offer and sale of such securities. Growth in the MBS markets has been significant over the past 20 years. For example, single-family MBS grew from less than $367 billion outstanding in 1981 to more than $3.3 trillion outstanding at the end of 2001, an 800% increase.[3] During this period, MBS have evolved, as have the standard disclosures made to investors. In order to understand the reasons for evaluating disclosure practices in the MBS markets, it is helpful to understand the development and operation of the MBS markets.

As described in this section, the MBS markets consist primarily of the MBS issued or guaranteed by two government-sponsored enterprises, Fannie Mae and Freddie Mac, and one United States-owned corporation, Ginnie Mae. MBS are also issued by private-label issuers, which are private institutions. The GSEs and Ginnie Mae guarantee payments on their respective MBS, whereas private-label issuers use various forms of credit enhancement.

The most commonly issued MBS are pass-through securities, which consist almost entirely of GSE and Ginnie Mae MBS, and REMICs, which are the primary security issued by private-label issuers. The MBS investor base has evolved, but remains largely institutional. The most important risks in the MBS market are prepayment risk and credit risk.[4] Investors perceive these risks differently depending on whether the issuer (or guarantor) is a GSE, Ginnie Mae, or private-label issuer, due to the different underlying mortgage loans and credit structures. This section includes a discussion of how these risks drive disclosures in the MBS markets. Other sections of this report discuss whether MBS disclosures can be enhanced.

A. Issuers

Fannie Mae, Freddie Mac, and Ginnie Mae were all created by federal law to address perceived deficiencies in the U.S. housing finance market.[5] The statutory

---

[3] 2 INSIDE MORTGAGE FINANCE PUBLICATIONS, INC., THE 2002 MORTGAGE MARKET STATISTICAL ANNUAL, 107 (2002).

[4] Interest rate risk, among other market risks, is another important risk for MBS investors to consider. However, because interest rate risk is not a disclosure issue specific only to the MBS, it is not separately addressed in this report.

[5] The enactment in 1934 of the National Housing Act established the Federal Housing Administration ("FHA"), which was to provide for the insurance of home mortgage loans made by private lenders in order to help facilitate home ownership. This statute also provided for the chartering of national mortgage associations. The only association ever formed, the National Mortgage Association of Washington, was created in 1938 and eventually became known as Fannie Mae. In 1968, Fannie Mae was split into two entities. One part retained the name Fannie Mae, was separated from FHA and became an investor-owned company. The other part, Ginnie Mae, became a wholly-owned government corporation within the auspices of the Department of Housing and Urban Development. In 1970, Congress passed the Emergency Home Finance Act of 1970 (12 U.S.C.§§ 1451-1459), chartering Freddie Mac. Freddie Mac was originally

purposes of the GSEs and Ginnie Mae are to facilitate a secondary market for residential mortgage loans and to enhance liquidity in such loans. The GSEs and Ginnie Mae enhance liquidity by enabling lenders and originators to sell their mortgage loans and use the proceeds from the sales to make new mortgage loans.

Fannie Mae was originally authorized only to buy FHA insured loans. After being split into two entities in 1968, Fannie Mae and Ginnie Mae, Fannie Mae was authorized to buy a broader range of loans. Freddie Mac was initially authorized to purchase conventional mortgages from federally insured financial institutions. Both Fannie Mae and Freddie Mac are now investor owned companies, and the common stock of both companies is traded on the New York Stock Exchange.

In 1992, OFHEO was established as an independent entity within the United States Department of Housing and Urban Development by the Federal Housing Enterprises Financial Safety and Soundness Act of 1992.[6] OFHEO's primary mission is ensuring the capital adequacy and financial safety and soundness of Fannie Mae and Freddie Mac.

Ginnie Mae does not buy or sell loans or issue MBS; instead, it guarantees payment on MBS that are backed by federally insured or guaranteed loans, mostly loans insured by the FHA and guaranteed by the Department of Veterans Affairs (the "VA"). Other guarantors or insurers of loans eligible as collateral for Ginnie Mae MBS include other offices in the Department of Housing and Urban Development ("HUD"), and the Department of Agriculture's Rural Housing Service. Ginnie Mae is a wholly-owned government corporation under the auspices of HUD.

Private-label issuers include commercial banks, savings associations, mortgage companies, investment banking firms and other entities that acquire and package mortgage loans for resale as MBS.[7]

B. MBS Investors

The types of investors in MBS have changed over time. Initially the primary purchasers of MBS were thrift institutions, commercial banks, insurance companies, pension funds, and mutual funds. More recently Fannie Mae, Freddie Mac, and international institutions have also become much more active market participants.[8] The

---

capitalized by the Federal Home Loan banks and controlled by the Federal Home Loan Bank Board. It was restructured under the Financial Institutions Reform, Recovery and Enforcement Act of 1989 and is now wholly-owned by private investors.

[6] *See* 12 U.S.C. §§4501-4641.

[7] *See* KENNETH G. LORE & CAMERON L. COWAN, MORTGAGE-BACKED SECURITIES; DEVELOPMENTS AND TRENDS IN THE SECONDARY MARKET 2-39 (2001).

[8] The GSEs together hold more MBS than any other individual investors in the market. The GSEs generally hold MBS in their portfolios until they mature. Banks hold more aggregate whole loans and MBS combined than the GSEs do. *See Guide to US Mortgage Backed Securities*, MBS RESEARCH (Deutsche Bank)(Jan. 2002) at 10 [hereinafter *Deutsche Bank Report*].

investor base remains overwhelmingly institutional. Investments in MBS are made for a variety of reasons. Some investors purchase MBS to hold long-term in portfolios while others purchase for short term trading purposes. MBS are also widely used for hedging purposes. Much of the development of GSE, Ginnie Mae, and private-label MBS markets has been in direct response to investor interests and demands.

C. Mortgage-Backed Securities

The MBS market as we know it today can be traced back to 1970, when Ginnie Mae first guaranteed a pool of mortgage loans. The creation of Freddie Mac in 1970 helped to expand the market.[9] Freddie Mac issued its first mortgage-backed participation certificates in 1971, and Fannie Mae issued its first MBS in 1981.[10] Private-label MBS issuance began in 1977 when Bank of America engaged in the first private-label issuance of interests in a trust that held single-family mortgages.[11] There was little private-label issuance from 1977 until the early 1980s.[12]

In the basic MBS structure, a group of mortgage loans is sold to a trust or other investment vehicle. In the case of residential home mortgages, the pools usually include a large enough number of loans so that information on no one loan is important in analyzing the pool. The investment vehicle owns the mortgage loans, issues securities that are either backed by or represent interests in the loans, and makes payments to investors out of the payments made on the loans. A servicer is hired to collect the mortgage payments from the borrowers and to pass the payments, less fees, including guarantee and trustee fees, through to the trustee, who passes these payments on to the investors that hold the MBS.

To facilitate sales of MBS, the GSEs and Ginnie Mae are authorized to guarantee the MBS. Thus, if for some reason, there is insufficient money to cover the payments due on the MBS, the GSEs make the payments due on the MBS. Ginnie Mae's guarantee arises if the issuer (typically the loan originator) does not make the delinquent payments to the MBS holders. Unlike Fannie Mae and Freddie Mac, which are permitted to issue, as well as guarantee the payments on, MBS, Ginnie Mae only guarantees the payment of MBS that are created by private entities. Ginnie Mae's guarantee of the payment of MBS

---

[9] *See* LORE & COWAN, *supra* note 7 at 1-10.

[10] *See* Linda Lowell, *Mortgage Pass-Through Securities in* THE HANDBOOK OF MORTGAGE-BACKED SECURITIES 25, 29 (Frank Fabozzi ed., 5th ed. 2001); Freddie Mac, *Key Corporate Statistics* (visited Dec. 12, 2002) < http://www.freddiemac.com/corporate/news/corp_stats.html>; Federal National Mortgage Association, SEC No-Action Letter (Nov. 7, 1977). *See also* Leland Brendsel, *Securitization's Role in Housing Finance: The Special Contributions of the Government Sponsored Enterprises in* A PRIMER ON SECURITIZATION 17, 17-29 (Leon T. Kendall et al. eds., 1997).

[11] *See* Bank of America Nat'l Trust & Savings Association, SEC No-Action Letter (Apr. 19, 1977). *See generally* Edward L. Pittman, *Economic and Regulatory Developments Affecting Mortgage Related Securities*, 64 NOTRE DAME L. REV. 497, 499 (1989).

[12] *See* LORE & COWAN, *supra* note 7, at 1-11;. Joseph Philip Forte, *Capital Markets Mortgage* (Apr. 1999)) <http://www.capitalconsortium.org/docs/capmarkm/htm>("While some isolated Private Label MBS issuance occurred in the late 1970s, non-GSE securitization of whole loans did not gain momentum until the thrift industry crises in the high interest rate environment of the early 1980s.").

is backed by the full faith and credit of the United States, whereas the guarantee obligations of Fannie Mae and Freddie Mac are not.[13]

There are significant differences in the composition and structure of typical private-label MBS compared to MBS issued or guaranteed by the GSEs or Ginnie Mae. The perceived strength of the guarantees, the evolution of tax law, and the demands of investors in an increasingly complex marketplace have contributed to current practices and product distinctions between GSE and Ginnie Mae MBS and private-label MBS. A number of regulatory and tax constraints initially impeded private entities from expanding into the MBS market created by the GSEs and Ginnie Mae.

1. Secondary Mortgage Market Enhancement Act of 1984

Many of the regulatory constraints affecting private entities were removed in 1984 with the passage of the Secondary Mortgage Market Enhancement Act of 1984 ("SMMEA"). SMMEA was intended to encourage private sector participation in the secondary mortgage market by, among other things, relaxing certain regulatory burdens that affected the ability of private-label issuers to sell their MBS.[14] For example, SMMEA allowed state and federally regulated financial institutions to invest in privately issued mortgage related securities.

2. Effect of Tax Laws on MBS Markets

Tax law constraints also affected the types of MBS that could be sold. Until the passage of the Tax Reform Act of 1986 ("1986 Tax Act"), which recognized the Real Estate Mortgage Investment Conduit ("REMIC") structure with its beneficial tax treatment, most MBS were sold as "pass-through" securities. As discussed below, pass-through securities pay an investor principal and interest received from payments on the mortgage loans that are the assets of the trust. The payments on the mortgage loans are passed through the trust to the investors as they are made.

Before 1986, the effect of the limitation on activity of grantor trusts under the tax laws restricted the use of trusts with multiple classes of securities with differing payment characteristics. In the multi-class structure, the principal and interest payments are not

---

[13] Payments on mortgage loans underlying Ginnie Mae MBS are federally insured or guaranteed.
Although the obligations of Fannie Mae and Freddie Mac are not federally guaranteed, a number of special statutory provisions have had the effect that lenders and investors provide the GSEs more ready access to lower cost funding than other issuers. Among these provisions are congressional charters, exemption from state and local income taxes, treatment of GSE securities as government securities under federal securities laws and the authority of the Secretary of the Treasury to purchase up to $2.25 billion of securities from each of Fannie Mae and Freddie Mac. *See also* the Federal Housing Enterprises Financial Safety and Soundness Act of 1992, 12 U.S.C. § 4501.

[14] The legislation was aimed at encouraging participation in the secondary mortgage market by investment banks, investment entities, mortgage bankers, private mortgage insurance companies, pension funds and other investors, depositary institutions and federal credit unions. *See* LORE & COWAN, *supra* note 7, at 1-14. *See also* Pittman, *supra* note 11; *infra* note 64.

just passed through pro rata as paid to all investors, but rather are divided into varying payment streams to create classes with different expected maturities, different levels of seniority or subordination or other differing characteristics. Prior to 1986, the tax law treated these multi-class trusts as associations taxable as corporations, and distributions would have been taxable at the trust level and also at the trust investor level. This "double taxation" made multi-class structures generally unfeasible.

The 1986 Tax Act eliminated the double taxation for multi-class vehicles structured as REMICs. With the advent of the REMIC, more complex structures with multiple classes were developed which divided up the payment streams on the mortgage loans that were collateral for the securities repayment obligations to investors.

3. Types of Underlying Mortgage Loans

There are differences between the GSE and Ginnie Mae MBS and private-label MBS in the composition of the mortgage loans comprising the collateral for the respective pools. The types of underlying mortgage loans that are eligible to be included in GSE and Ginnie Mae MBS affect the composition of pools backing private-label MBS because originators can generally receive the best price for eligible loans in GSE and Ginnie Mae transactions.[15] Eligibility is not the sole criterion, however. Because the GSEs require a higher fee to accept some loans of lesser credit quality, sometimes originators may find a private-label transaction more attractive.

The mortgage loans included in Fannie Mae and Freddie Mac MBS generally have the following characteristics:

- mortgages are on residential properties, most commonly one to four family homes (these are referred to as single family loans);
- mortgages are generally 15 year and 30 year maturities that are fully amortizing;[16]
- most mortgage loans are fixed rate;[17]
- most mortgages have monthly payments;
- there typically are no prepayment penalties;
- the loans are due on sale of the underlying property and cannot be assumed by the buyer of the property;[18]
- mortgage loans must be within the "conforming loan limit", which for one-unit homes in 2003 is $322,700.[19]

---

[15] *See* Lowell, *supra* note 10, at 31-32 ("Normally it is more profitable for originators of conforming loans… to use the agency programs").

[16] There are some 10 year, 20 year and balloon (not fully amortizing or short maturity) loans, among others, that are securitized as well.

[17] There are also adjustable rate mortgages that can be securitized as Fannie Mae or Freddie Mac MBS.

[18] FHA and VA loans that might be part of a Ginnie Mae security can be assumed by a subsequent buyer of the property.

[19] A loan that is a single-family loan within the loan limit that is set annually for Fannie Mae and Freddie Mac is said to be within the conforming loan limit. There is no similar limit on the size of loans guaranteed

- loans within the conforming loan limit generally satisfy other GSE specifications for loan documentation, credit information and property type, among other requirements.[20]

There are some mortgage loans made to borrowers with good credit histories that are within the conforming loan limit but do not satisfy all the standard GSE underwriting guidelines, including documentation, for mortgage loans. These mortgage loans are called "Alternative A" or "Alt A" loans. These Alt A loans fail to satisfy the GSE guidelines for reasons such as limited or low documentation of income from the borrower (for reasons of speed or convenience to the borrower), unstable income sources, higher loan-to-value ratios ("LTV") or other ratios of payments to income.[21]

Alternative A loans and some lower credit quality loans that are within the conforming loan limit can be swapped for Fannie Mae or Freddie Mac MBS or pooled and sold as private-label MBS. Fannie Mae or Freddie Mac will issue MBS backed by such loans if the lender pays a higher guarantee fee that compensates the GSE for the potentially higher risk.

Apart from Alt A loans, there are other types of mortgage loans that do not satisfy standard GSE requirements. Mortgage loans that are larger than the conforming loan limit, called jumbo loans, cannot, by statute, be included in GSE or Ginnie Mae MBS pools. Mortgage loans are also made to borrowers who fail to meet GSE underwriting requirements because of certain borrower or loan characteristics. For example, mortgage loans made to borrowers with poor credit histories or high debt-to-income ratios may be ineligible for securitization by the GSEs or eligible only by payment of a higher guarantee fee. These are the types of loans that typically comprise the pools backing the private-label MBS.

Under the Ginnie Mae MBS program, HUD-approved mortgage originators pool FHA, VA or certain other federally-insured mortgages into MBS and sell the MBS guaranteed by Ginnie Mae. The terms of the underlying mortgage loans must comply with the underwriting requirements of the FHA or VA, as applicable.

As a result of the GSE underwriting criteria and conforming loan limits and FHA and VA underwriting requirements which do not apply to private-label issuers, the mortgage loans in private-label MBS generally have more diverse collateral, credit risk or other underwriting characteristics than GSE or Ginnie Mae MBS and have wider variances in a number of terms including interest rate, term, size, purpose and borrower characteristics. Private-label pools more frequently include second mortgages, high loan-

---

by Ginnie Mae, but the underwriting guidelines of the federal housing programs may directly or indirectly establish such limits. For example, the FHA has an established maximum family home mortgage limit of $280,749. U.S. Department of Housing and Urban Development, *HUD Announces Higher FHA Home Loan Limits to Help More American Families Become Homeowners* (last modified Jan. 2, 2003) <http://www.hud.gov/news/release.cfm?content=pr03-001.cfm>.

[20] *See generally Deutsche Bank Report, supra* note 8 at 8.

[21] *See* FRANK J. FABOZZI & JOHN N. DUNLEVY, REAL ESTATE-BACKED SECURITIES 98-99 (2001).

to-value mortgages and manufactured housing loans. The coupon rates and maturities of the underlying mortgage loans in a private-label MBS pool may vary to a greater extent than those included in a GSE guaranteed pool.

4. Guarantees or Credit Enhancement

As noted above, the GSEs and Ginnie Mae guarantee payments to investors on their MBS. This guarantee ensures that investors receive scheduled payments of principal and interest, regardless of whether payments on the underlying mortgages are made. MBS issued in the private-label market are typically not guaranteed by the issuer and instead rely on other forms of credit enhancement or support to give investors greater assurance they will receive payments on their MBS. The credit enhancement in private-label MBS may be internal or external to the vehicle issuing the security. External credit enhancements generally involve insurance or a letter of credit purchased by private-label issuers to support the underlying mortgage payments.[22] Internal credit supports, reserve funds, or senior-subordinated structures are structural features of multi-class MBS, such as REMICs, that are designed to help ensure repayment to more senior classes of securities before other subordinated classes in the case of default of the underlying mortgage loans.[23]

The most common credit enhancement currently used in private-label MBS is the senior-subordinated structure in REMICs. In the senior-subordinated credit enhancement, the trust will issue different classes of securities. There will be a senior class or tranche and at least one class that has a subordinated right of payment to the senior class. The senior class, which bears the least amount of risk of default of the underlying mortgages, will carry a lower interest rate. The subordinated class, which bears the greatest amount of risk of default of the underlying mortgage loans, will carry a higher interest rate in order to compensate for the greater risk exposure. The level of credit protection this structure provides to the senior class may decline over time due to prepayments and thus other mechanisms, such as prepayments going disproportionately to the senior class (known as shifting interest structures), must be in place to provide further safeguards.[24] Because the senior-subordinated credit enhancement relies on a multi-class security structure, this form of credit enhancement is typically available for REMIC or other multi-class MBS, and not pass-through MBS.

5. Risks – Prepayment and Credit

a. Prepayment Risk

The most significant feature and risk that all MBS share is prepayment risk, which is the risk that principal payments on an underlying loan will be paid earlier or later than

---

[22] *See* Frank J. Fabozzi et al., *Nonagency CMOs* in THE HANDBOOK OF MORTGAGE-BACKED SECURITIES, *supra* note 10, at 267, 268.
[23] *See Id.* at 268-69.
[24] *See* FABOZZI & DUNLEVY, *supra* note 21, at 73.

expected. Unscheduled prepayments may affect the return realized by MBS investors. When an investor purchases an MBS or any other fixed income security, the investor does so with the understanding that the price he or she is paying for the security reflects uncertainty about its expected life. Prepayment risk on MBS is influenced by a wide range of factors that relate both to general market conditions, including interest rates, and the performance on individual loans included in the portfolio of loans backing an MBS issuance.

Prepayments arise for two primary reasons – refinancing and moving. As interest rates fall below rates on existing mortgages, borrowers may, and commonly do, prepay their existing loans and refinance at lower rates. Refinancings are recognized as being the primary driver of prepayments.[25] Prepayments also occur when homeowners sell their homes. Most mortgage loans must be paid in full when a home is sold. The mortgage loan can also be paid prior to its due date or maturity if the homeowner does not pay the loan and the lender repossesses or forecloses on and sells the home. Finally, a borrower may prepay a loan, in whole or in part, at any time for any other reason. When MBS prepay as a result of borrower refinancing, investors seeking to reinvest in the fixed income market will generally be forced to make a new investment in a lower interest rate environment. When prepayments are slower than expected, it often means that interest rates have risen. The security pays later than expected, and the investor cannot take advantage of more attractive investment opportunities with those funds.[26]

b. Credit Risk

The potentially significant risk to investors in private-label MBS that is generally thought by investors to be less significant in the case of GSE and Ginnie Mae MBS is credit risk. Investors in MBS, as with other fixed income instruments, evaluate the risk of whether they will receive the scheduled payments of principal and interest on their MBS. Credit risk reflects the risk that the borrowers on the underlying loans may not be able to make timely payments on the loans or may even default on the loans.

In the absence of a guarantee or external credit enhancement, MBS investors generally can look only to the assets or collateral of the trust, the underlying mortgage loans, as the source of payments on their securities and to the structure of the transaction for any internal credit enhancement. The creditworthiness of the underlying borrowers becomes significantly more relevant in private-label MBS offerings because there is seldom an entity that is guaranteeing the payment of the securities. Therefore, if the borrowers do not pay the mortgage loans, the MBS securities will not pay, absent some credit enhancement. Consequently, GSE and Ginnie Mae MBS and the private-label MBS may pose differing degrees of risk for investors.

---

[25] *See* Michael Bykhovsky, *Overview of Recent Prepayment Behavior and Advances in Modeling in* THE HANDBOOK OF MORTGAGE-BACKED SECURITIES, *supra* note 10, at 365, 372.
[26] *See* LORE & COWAN *supra* note 7, at 3-5; Lowell, *supra* note 10, at 35-42.

Since the GSEs and Ginnie Mae guarantee the timely payment of principal and interest on the MBS, a GSE and Ginnie Mae MBS investor looks to the GSEs and Ginnie Mae to determine the credit risk. Ginnie Mae's guarantee is the full faith and credit guarantee of the United States. In contrast, Fannie Mae's and Freddie Mac's guarantees are based solely on their own credit quality. Fannie Mae and Freddie Mac provide extensive corporate disclosure and will soon register their common stock under the Exchange Act, subjecting the two companies to all of the disclosure requirements of the federal securities laws. Investors in Fannie Mae and Freddie Mac MBS may look to these disclosures to assess those companies' abilities to fulfill the guarantees of the MBS. Investors may also look to information provided by OFHEO about the GSEs' creditworthiness, including results of examinations and risk based capital stress tests.

In addition to assessing the credit quality of the underlying mortgage loans, investors in private-label MBS must look to the creditworthiness of the provider of the external credit enhancement or must evaluate the reliability of the transaction structure to provide any internal credit enhancement and the reliability of a rating agency's rating. The amount of disclosure private-label issuers must provide with respect to third party credit enhancements varies with the type and level of support expected. Private-label issuers are required to discuss in their registration statements the material terms of any credit enhancement, whether internal or external and to provide information regarding the credit enhancer, insurer or guarantor.[27]

D. Structure of the MBS

As noted above, the most common form of private-label MBS is in the form of a REMIC. The other common form of MBS is the pass-through security, which is used predominantly by the GSEs and Ginnie Mae. Both structures are briefly summarized below.

1. Pass-Through Securities

The most common type of MBS is a pass-through security backed by a pool of single-family mortgage loans. Generally, pass-through MBS are created by pooling or packaging mortgage loans together in a trust or other collective investment vehicle and selling the interests in the trust.[28] In the pass-through structure, the certificate holders

---

[27] For example, where insurance is obtained on the pool backing the private-label MBS, the material terms of the insurance or guarantee and information on the insurer or guarantor must be described in the prospectus supplement. If the pool insurance or other third party credit enhancement insures or guarantees payments on 20% or more of the cash flows of the MBS vehicle, the registration statement must include audited financial statements of the party providing the insurance or credit enhancement. If the third party enhancement is a guarantee of the MBS rather than the pool cash flows, the guarantee is also a security that either must be registered under the Securities Act or exempt from registration. The insurance itself is exempt from registration under the Securities Act under Section 3(a)(8). *See* 15 U.S.C. § 77c(a)(8). Even if the guarantee or insurance is exempt from registration, disclosure relating to the financial condition of the guarantor is required.

[28] "Pass through certificates generally are treated as a sale of the mortgage loans to the holders of the participation certificates for tax and accounting purposes." LORE & COWAN, *supra* note 7, at 3-9.

own undivided interests in the pool. All payments on the underlying mortgage loans, including principal, scheduled interest, and unscheduled prepayments are passed through, on a pro rata basis, to the holders of the pool interest or participation certificates after deducting the servicing fees, Ginnie Mae and GSE guarantee fees, and trust expenses. The assets of the trust or other vehicle are the mortgage loans in the pool. Most pass-through vehicles own fixed rate mortgages, although adjustable rate mortgages may also be assets of a pass-through MBS entity.[29] The coupon or interest rate payable on a pass-through MBS is less than the interest rate payable on the underlying mortgage loans in the pool. The interest differential is used to pay for the guarantee fee to one of the GSEs and the servicing fee to the servicer. Generally, the underlying mortgage loans are serviced by the originating lender or another institution that has bought the servicing rights.[30]

Private-label issuers can, but in most cases do not, issue pass-through securities. In a private-label MBS, the interest differential would be used to pay for credit enhancement or credit support, the servicing fee to the servicer, and trust expenses.

2. REMICs

As previously noted, the REMIC is a multiple-class security vehicle that does not have the burden of double taxation. The assets underlying the REMIC securities can be either other MBS or whole mortgage loans. The assets are pooled and cash flows from the assets are distributed to the various REMIC security classes according to the priorities specified in advance. The REMIC structure allows issuers to create securities with short, intermediate and long-term maturities. This flexibility enables issuers to expand the market for the MBS to fit the needs of a variety of investors, not just investors looking for 30-year fixed-rate securities. The REMIC structure has allowed for a broader group of investors. REMICs may also be used to address particular investment objectives or concerns about prepayment risk by carving up principal and interest payments on the underlying mortgage loans to create different timing and levels of payments on the securities.[31]

REMICs are issued by private-label issuers and under the GSE and Ginnie Mae programs. Fannie Mae and Freddie Mac REMICs generally are backed by GSE MBS.

---

[29] Fannie Mae, Freddie Mac and Ginnie Mae issue pass-through MBS backed by adjustable rate mortgages. *See* Fannie Mae, *Understanding Fannie Mae MBS* (visited Dec. 12, 2002) <http://www fanniemae.com/markets/mbssecurities/about_mbs/understanding_mbs/mbs_selecting.jhtml?p =Mortgage-Backed+Securities&s=Understanding+Fannie+Mae+MBS&t=Selecting+an+MBS +Investment>; Freddie Mac, *About PCs* (visited Dec.12,2002)<http://www freddiemac.com/mbs/html/aop _gold html>.

[30] "The servicer collects all payments of principal and interest from individual mortgagors and is responsible for enforcing payment of delinquent loans and reporting to the security holders." LORE & COWAN, *supra* note 7, at 3-9. There appears to be a growing trend toward unbundling the servicing activities from the loan origination activities and consolidation within the servicing industry. *See id.*

[31] *See generally* Lehman Brothers Inc. Mortgage Research Group, *Collateralized Mortgage Obligations in* THE HANDBOOK OF MORTGAGE-BACKED SECURITIES, *supra* note 10, at 169, 169-196.

The GSEs then guarantee the payment obligations on the REMIC securities. In the Ginnie Mae REMIC program, Ginnie Mae guarantees the timely payment of principal and interest on each of the classes. Ginnie Mae REMICs are pools of Ginnie Mae guaranteed certificates.

Due to the widely diverse coupon and payment characteristics of the underlying mortgage loans, most private-label securities are structured as REMICs.[32] Private-label REMICs are generally backed by jumbo or otherwise non-conforming mortgage loans. The GSE participation in the REMIC market has effectively priced most potential private-label REMIC securities backed by conforming loans out of the market. This is because, as a result of the GSE or Ginnie Mae guarantee, investors will likely pay more for GSE and Ginnie Mae securities backed by the same loans, even though guarantee fees are paid from the pool cash flows.

In a standard REMIC structure, known as sequential pay, each class or tranche of the security is generally paid the coupon rate on a monthly basis. Principal is paid on the regular classes in sequential order: senior classes are paid first, and then the subordinated classes. Any prepayments are allocated in the same way. The effect of prepayments is that more senior classes may be paid off much sooner or later than anticipated. Prepayments to senior classes can also shorten the expected maturities of later maturity classes in a sequential pay structure, but later maturities have less prepayment risk than exists for securities in a pass-through structure.

E. Creation and Sales of GSE and Ginnie Mae MBS

1. Creation of GSE and Ginnie Mae MBS

GSE and Ginnie Mae MBS are created through a variety of programs. For Fannie Mae and Freddie Mac guaranteed MBS, each GSE has two basic mechanisms to create MBS – a "cash" program and a "swap" program. A mortgage originator selects a group of mortgage loans that it determines to sell to one of the GSEs as a package. Under the "swap" programs, the lender selects and pools a group of conforming mortgage loans that meet the GSE underwriting standards and "swaps" them for MBS issued and guaranteed by one of the GSEs representing interests in that same pool of mortgages. Under their "cash" programs, Fannie Mae and Freddie Mac take whole mortgage loans and give the originators cash back. Subsequently, the GSE will decide which mortgages out of the pools it has purchased in the cash program to pool and use as collateral for new GSE MBS or whether to hold the mortgage loans as an investment. The GSE will then issue MBS backed by the loans it has purchased from lenders or originators, guarantee the timely payment of principal and interest on the securities and sell the MBS through dealers. The mortgage originator, not the GSE, decides whether to swap the loans for MBS or to receive cash. A small amount of Fannie Mae and Freddie Mac MBS are created through their respective "cash" programs, with the vast majority being created

---

[32] *See* FABOZZI & DUNLEVY, *supra* note 21, at 65-66.

through their respective "swap" programs. The loan originator, of course, would also be free to use the loans in a private-label MBS issuance.

Under the Ginnie Mae MBS program, a HUD-approved mortgage loan originator pools FHA, VA or certain other federally-insured mortgages and sells MBS guaranteed by Ginnie Mae. Ginnie Mae does not issue securities or own the underlying assets but rather guarantees the payment of the securities backed by the underlying mortgage loans or mortgage pools. Like the loans in the Fannie Mae and Freddie Mac swaps, the loans in the mortgage pools comprising Ginnie Mae guaranteed MBS are chosen by the lender, not by Ginnie Mae.[33] Ginnie Mae has pool and disclosure guidelines establishing the permissible content of the pools and required disclosures including the number of issuers, first payment date, maturity, and number of loans.[34]

The GSEs have other MBS products that are either larger pass-through structures, which can be pools of pools (small balance pools consolidated into one larger pool) or are collateralized mortgage obligations such as REMICs.

2. The To-Be-Announced Market

In addition to the differences in the collateral and structures discussed above, private-label MBS are sold to investors through different market mechanisms than are GSE and Ginnie Mae MBS.[35]

Most pass-through MBS of each of Fannie Mae, Freddie Mac and Ginnie Mae are eligible to be sold in the "to-be-announced" or TBA market, which is essentially a forward or delayed delivery market.[36] Only pass-through securities issued or guaranteed by Fannie Mae, Freddie Mac or Ginnie Mae and comprised of single-family mortgages are eligible for trading in the TBA market. The TBA market allows mortgage lenders essentially to sell the loans they intend to fund even before the loans are closed. This also allows the lender to lock in an interest rate for the borrower. The lender, or other market

---

[33] *See* LORE & COWAN, *supra* note 7, at 2-6.

[34] Ginnie Mae has two basic types of securities: Ginnie Mae I and Ginnie Mae II. The Ginnie Mae I product is comprised only of pools formed by a single issuer, pays principal and interest separately on the certificates, and the underlying mortgages have the same interest rate. The Ginnie Mae II product may have pools formed by single or multiple issuers, has an aggregate principal and interest payment on the certificates, and the interest rates on the underlying loans may vary within a specified percentage range.

[35] While historically the MBS market has been a dealer to dealer or dealer to customer market with trades occurring based on telephone discussions and fax, the growth of electronic trading platforms has impacted the TBA market. The growth of these electronic trading platforms has been noted to result in greater transparency in TBA pricing as well as improved efficiency and accessibility. The interdealer market now depends heavily on electronic trading. In 2002 there were 12 electronic systems that covered the MBS market. *See* The Bond Market Association, *e-Commerce in the Fixed Income Markets – The 2002 Review of Electronic Transaction Systems*, at 4-7 (last modified Nov. 2002)<http://www.bondmarkets.com/research/ETSRpt1102.pdf>.

[36] Other GSE MBS, including REMICs are sold in the same manner as other fixed income instruments in the over the counter market, which involves dealer to dealer or dealer to investor communications and negotiation through interdealer screens, by telephone, e-mail or fax.

participant, will enter into a forward contract to sell MBS in the TBA market, promising to deliver MBS on the settlement date sometime in the future. In the TBA market, GSE and Ginnie Mae MBS are traded on a forward or delayed delivery basis with settlement up to 180 days later. The actual mortgage pools comprising the MBS are not specified at the time of sale. In fact, many of the mortgage loans may not even be signed (and the mortgage pools created) at the time of sale. The largest volume of trading in the TBA market is for settlement within 30 days.[37]

In a TBA trade the seller and buyer agree to five pieces of information before entering into the transaction: the type of security, which will usually be a certain type of Fannie Mae, Freddie Mac or Ginnie Mae program and type of mortgage (*i.e.*, GNMA 30-year pass-throughs); coupon or interest rate; face value (the total dollar amount of MBS the purchaser wishes); price; and settlement date. The purchaser will contract to acquire a specified dollar amount of MBS, which may be satisfied when the seller delivers one or more MBS pools at settlement. Forty-eight hours before settlement, the seller specifies or allocates the identity and number of mortgage pools by the specific pool numbers and CUSIPs to be delivered to satisfy the TBA trade.

The Bond Market Association, a private trade association of dealers in debt securities, publishes guidelines governing the mechanics of trading and settling MBS, which are intended to implement standard industry practices. The guidelines, titled "Uniform Practices for the Clearance and Settlement of Mortgage-Backed Securities and Other Related Securities," contain specific guidelines for trading and settling GSE and Ginnie Mae pass-through MBS in the TBA market, known as Good Delivery Guidelines.[38] The Good Delivery Guidelines outline the basic terms and conditions for trading, confirming, delivering and settling MBS. The Good Delivery Guidelines set forth the basic characteristics that GSE and Ginnie Mae pass-through MBS must have to be able to be delivered to settle an open TBA transaction. Most newly issued GSE and Ginnie Mae pass-through MBS are eligible to be sold in the TBA market. Already outstanding GSE and Ginnie Mae pass-through MBS may also be used to cover a TBA trade. Therefore, the mortgage originator has until 48 hours before the settlement date to decide whether to use new pools of mortgages or to buy outstanding GSE or Ginnie Mae MBS to cover the trade. The Task Force understands that roughly 75% of GSE and Ginnie Mae MBS are eligible to trade in the TBA market.[39]

---

[37] *See generally* Jeffrey Biby, Srinivas Modukuri & Brian Hargrave, *Trading, Settlement and Clearing Procedures for Agency MBS in* THE HANDBOOK OF MORTGAGE-BACKED SECURITIES, *supra* note 10, at 105, 105-14.

[38] *See* THE BOND MARKET ASSOCIATION, UNIFORM PRACTICES FOR THE CLEARANCE AND SETTLEMENT OF MORTGAGE-BACKED SECURITIES AND OTHER RELATED SECURITIES (1990) [hereinafter UNIFORM PRACTICES]. Fixed Income Clearing Corporation, the successor to the MBS Clearing Corporation, a clearing agency registered with the Commission, provides clearing and settlement services for GSE and Ginnie Mae MBS transactions.

[39] Trading is done by phone, fax or online. Online or other electronic sites openly display bids, thus making the trade process more transparent. An increasing amount of GSE and Ginnie Mae MBS are being traded online. According to the Bond Market Association, approximately $69 billion of GSE MBS are traded every day including $20 billion to $25 billion of TBAs. Of these, TradeWeb, an online trading platform, estimates that nearly $3 billion of those TBAs are traded on its platform, which lets institutions

The Good Delivery Guidelines were developed as a result of the unique nature of the GSE and Ginnie Mae MBS market. The TBA market developed in response to the demands of market participants for more liquidity in trading GSE and Ginnie Mae MBS. In order for the market to work on a delayed delivery basis, with sales of GSE and Ginnie Mae MBS occurring before the underlying mortgage loans close, and to account for the potential that not all commitments for mortgage loans will close (called pipeline risk), the market had to develop a process that would allow the identification of the securities that would be delivered in satisfaction of a trade a very short time before settlement, rather than at the time the forward trade was entered into. In addition, because there are over 1 million individual GSE and Ginnie Mae MBS, with huge variations in outstanding principal amount, it was recognized that it was impractical and inefficient, and would greatly limit liquidity, and generally reduce price, to attempt to trade these GSE and Ginnie Mae MBS on a pool-by-pool basis. Thus, it was essential to establish a concept of fungibility or interchangeability among pools that would facilitate both forward trading and an orderly and liquid trading market in GSE and Ginnie Mae pass-through MBS.[40]

As a result of the GSE and Ginnie Mae standardized underwriting guidelines for single-family mortgages and the trading and settling parameters of the Good Delivery Guidelines, GSE MBS that may be delivered to satisfy a TBA trade will have similar characteristics. The mortgage loans underlying GSE and Ginnie Mae pass-through MBS are pooled together according to similar characteristics that are based on guidelines established by the GSEs and Ginnie Mae and enable the pools to satisfy the Good Delivery Guidelines.[41] Under the Good Delivery Guidelines, only GSE and Ginnie Mae pass-through MBS that are within a particular product type and coupon, have certain basic attributes and fall within certain parameters can be delivered to satisfy a TBA trade. The TBA market functions on the premise that even though each pool that will be created is unique, all pools eligible for delivery on a given TBA trade are equivalent in their characteristics and expected performance. Therefore, any distinct characteristics of the underlying mortgage loans comprising a pool delivered in a trade are considered to blend together so that the MBS they back can be considered a generic security. As a result, TBA market participants consider MBS of Fannie Mae, Freddie Mac and Ginnie Mae that meet the Good Delivery Guidelines to be interchangeable or fungible with other such MBS issued or guaranteed by Fannie Mae, Freddie Mac or Ginnie Mae, respectively.

TBA trading vastly improves the liquidity of TBA-eligible pass-through MBS. Market participants have noted that the fungible nature of TBA securities promotes broad liquidity, which adds to efficiencies in pricing, execution, delivery and settlement. In addition, the TBA market allows lenders to finance mortgages, thereby locking in interest

---

send out bond inquiries to dealers and offers mutual disclosure to both parties in a transaction. *See* Tommy Fernandez, *Street Warming to MBS Web Marketplaces*, AM. BANKER, Aug. 13, 2001, at 5.

[40] *See* Biby, Modukuri & Hargrave, *supra* note 37; *Deutsche Bank Report*, *supra* note 8, at 18. THE BOND MARKET ASSOCIATION, TBAS: TO-BE-ANNOUNCED MORTGAGE SECURITIES TRANSACTIONS (1999).

[41] Among the parameters in the Good Delivery Guidelines is a restriction on the percentage of non standard mortgage loans in an underlying pool that have diverging characteristics such as relocation loans, co-op loans and buy down loans (where a payment is made to reduce the interest rate.)

rates, prior to the actual closing of a mortgage.[42] Commentators have noted that "[w]ithout the TBA mechanism, mortgage pools could not be sold until they had been formed, and originators would have to hedge their pipelines using Treasury futures or Treasury or MBS options. Using TBA forward sales to hedge pipelines is more efficient and has probably resulted in lower mortgage rates for borrowers."[43]

The pricing of TBA-eligible MBS is based on the assumption that the GSE or Ginnie Mae MBS delivered in the TBA trade will be a generic MBS – one that, based on the information available, is considered to be part of a fungible universe of TBA-eligible MBS. In a TBA transaction, the security traded is the one that the seller can buy or obtain at the lowest cost for delivery at settlement (and thus has a higher profit potential). In other words, TBA prices are based on the GSE or Ginnie Mae pass-through MBS that are the "cheapest to deliver." Thus, the price of the cheapest to deliver security or the generic security in a TBA trade is the base price for TBA trades. Because the generic security trade price is the base price for TBA trades, this price is also the floor off which other MBS trades are priced. Any extra amount paid for a perceived benefit is measured relative to the base price. Market participants note that the tremendous market liquidity has created pricing efficiency and reduced the bid/ask spread to 1/16 of a point or even 1/32 of a point. Bloomberg LP and other third party vendors publish average daily price quotations for TBA trades, which include only generic securities. There is also a competitive dealer and interdealer broker network from which daily pricing of trades in generic securities is available.

As described above, the Good Delivery Guidelines establish standard notification and settlement dates for GSE and Ginnie Mae MBS. The trading guidelines require delivery of confirmations within one business day of the TBA forward trade. The confirmation must contain information regarding the security and the transaction, including product type, coupon rate and settlement month. The confirmation may contain other stipulated conditions that were negotiated as part of the trade. The Good Delivery

---

[42] "Other market participants that benefit from TBA trading are the mortgage bankers, commercial banks and thrifts that originate residential mortgages and sell them into the secondary mortgage market in securitized form. Most mortgage application processes allow a borrower to lock in a mortgage rate at some point prior to closing. After this rate lock, the mortgage originator is exposed to interest rate risk: the risk that the value of the mortgage may change as market rates change before the mortgage is sold. Actual MBS pools can be formed only after mortgages close; while they are in the pipeline, pool characteristics may shift if applicants withdraw their applications or postpone closing, fail to meet underwriting standards, or change loan amounts. Originators frequently hedge their pipelines of rate-locked mortgages by selling them into the forward market as mortgage securities for TBA delivery months (or more) in the future. TBA trading allows originators to sell prospective mortgage securities before they know the specific collateral characteristics of the pools." Biby, Modukuri & Hargrave, *supra* note 37, at 106.

[43] *Id*. Although attempts have been made to establish a mortgage futures contract, the most recent product by the Chicago Board of Trade introduced in 2001 was delisted in January 2002 due to lack of market interest. Market participants told the Task Force that they found mortgage futures not to be acceptable for a few reasons. First, the futures contracts did not afford participants the same flexibility or economic certainty they currently have in the TBA market. Second, the dealer community did not support the product.

Guidelines also address delivery and settlement.[44] Under the notification process of the guidelines, to satisfy the seller's delivery obligation regarding the TBA trade, a seller must notify a purchaser 48 hours before settlement of the specific pools that will be delivered and the manner in which the pools will be assigned or allocated. Allocation is the process by which the seller determines which GSE or Ginnie Mae MBS will be delivered to the buyer to satisfy good delivery and requires that GSE or Ginnie Mae MBS assigned pools must be within certain parameters. The parameters are necessary to maintain the fungible character of the MBS delivered to satisfy a TBA trade. These parameters include the permissible variance in the face value of MBS being delivered and the number of MBS pools per million dollars traded.[45] GSE and Ginnie Mae MBS are issued and transferred in book-entry form.

The Good Delivery Guidelines prohibit delivery of securities until 2 business days after the seller provides pool information. As discussed below, the dollar roll market enables sellers to acquire pools to deliver to avoid settlement fails or to follow buy-in requirements.

3. Types of Trades of TBA-Eligible MBS

TBA-eligible MBS may be traded three ways: generic, stipulated and specified trades. Generic TBA trades are trades that merely fit the Good Delivery Guidelines. The majority of GSE and Ginnie Mae pass-through MBS are traded on a generic basis through the TBA market process. Stipulated TBA trades are TBA-eligible securities meeting Good Delivery Guidelines that have characteristics that have been requested by the investor. In general, the stipulations are based on publicly available information about the pools or alterations of the Good Delivery Guidelines. The most common stipulated terms are number of pools that can be delivered, the principal dollar amount variance, maturity year, weighted average loan age of the mortgage loans in the pool, and geographic location of the underlying properties. Recently, investors have increasingly stipulated Alternative A characteristics. Investors also commonly stipulate to late delivery to facilitate a seller's ability to obtain pools to satisfy an investor's trade.

---

[44] "Bond Market Association scheduling of monthly settlements is designed to distribute settlement activity as evenly as possible over a series of days.... The monthly schedule was established for two main reasons. Dealers must await pool factors released near the beginning of the month before security trades can be settled. The factor is used to determine the current face value of securities. In addition, dealers can more easily create tradable blocks if all pools for a month of trading are specified on the same day; the larger the inventory of pools, the easier it is to meet the requirement of each buyer. Thus, the monthly settlement schedule helps ensure liquidity in the [GSE] MBS market." *Id.* at 107.

[45] Variance is the permitted deviation in the quantity of GSE MBS that can be delivered to satisfy an outstanding TBA obligation. The standard variance is currently .01% of the face value agreed to at the trade date. At settlement, therefore, a seller may deliver from 99.99% to 100.01% of the face amount of securities. The guidelines also mandate that TBA trades include a maximum of three pools per million for MBS with coupons below 11% and five pools per million for MBS with coupons of 11% or more.

The pools per million and variance rule are important both for combining irregular pools or securities and for ensuring that buyers are not forced to accept delivery of a large number of splintered pools. The notification rule gives the parties to the trade time to prepare for settlement and ensure that the trade goes smoothly. *See Id.* at 109-10.

Investors entering into a stipulated trade will pay a higher price than the price for a generic pool in the TBA market. This is known as "paying up." As with generic TBA trades, there is no specific security identified at the time the parties enter into the trade.[46]

Finally, TBA-eligible securities may be traded on a specified pool basis. Investors that wish to purchase a particular mortgage pool will engage in a specified trade – they will identify the actual pool they wish to purchase by pool and CUSIP number. Unlike generic and stipulated trades, specified pool trades occur outside the TBA market. There are a number of reasons an investor may engage in a specified trade. For instance, an investor may want to purchase particular pools that have been in existence for a period of time, known as seasoned MBS, because of their better known prepayment characteristics.[47] Investors can examine the prepayment history of seasoned pools before actually purchasing them. Although seasoned pools may trade in the TBA market, and can be used to settle any TBA trade, they often trade on a specified basis outside the TBA market because of the increased differentiation in prepayment histories.

Among newly created MBS, specified pools generally command the highest price due to the additional available information regarding the content of the pool indicating the pool is worth more than a generic pool. Market participants have indicated that investors generally obtain information on these pools from dealers or originators. These market participants have indicated, however, that certain historical information they may receive about previously specified pools cannot be independently verified.

4. Dollar Rolls

In addition to the flexibility the TBA market gives to buyers to determine the level of specificity the buyer desires in terms of pool characteristics, the TBA market has two distinct trading uses. Investors, dealers, originators and other participants use the TBA market not only to acquire pools for investment or to form other investment vehicles, but TBA market participants trade TBA pools in "dollar rolls" as financing vehicles.[48]

---

[46] According to The Bond Market Association stipulations could be on, among other things, date of issuance, geographic, lot, lot variance, maturity, pieces, pools per lot, pools per million, pools per trade, trade variance, weighted average coupon, loan age or maturity, whole pool, and year of issuance. *See* The Bond Market Association, *Fixed Income Protocols Initiative, TBA Mortgage-Backed Securities, Draft Business Practices Documentation in Plain English (working draft 2002)* 6 (visited Dec. 12, 2002) <http://www.bondmarkets.com/ecommerce/tba-mbs_business_practices.pdf>; Jordan & Jordan, *The Bond Market Association STP/T 1 Mortgage-Backed Securities & Related Products, Codes of Practice (working draft version 2.0 Dec. 19, 2001)* 5 (visited Dec. 12, 2002)<http://www.bondmarkets.com/ecommerce/cop_mortgage_draft_2-0.pdf>); *Deutsche Bank Report, supra* note 8, at 18. According to some market participants, mortgage originators are increasing stipulated pool formation, which increases variability in pool prepayment speeds.
[47] REMIC issuers that may be using GSE or Ginnie Mae MBS for the assets of their trust may need pools that have particular collateral characteristics and thus may specify pools for this purpose.
[48] *See Deutsche Bank Report, supra* note 8, at 32. *See generally* Biby, Modukuri & Hargrave *supra* note 37, at 139-148.

Dollar rolls, which are a form of collateralized short-term financing where the collateral consists of mortgage securities, perform a function analogous to that provided by the repo (repurchase agreement) market. The vast majority of financing in the MBS market occurs through the dollar roll market, which takes advantage of the flexibility of the TBA market. Unlike a reverse repurchase agreement, which generally requires redelivery of exactly the same securities that are delivered during the first leg of the transaction, a dollar roll is a simultaneous purchase and sale of substantially similar (TBA) securities for different settlement dates. The dealer, who is said to "roll in" the securities received, is not required to deliver the identical securities, only securities that meet the Good Delivery Guidelines. Thus, the investor may assume some risk because the characteristics of the MBS delivered to the investor may be less favorable than the MBS the investor delivered to the dealer. Because the dealer is not obligated to return the identical MBS collateral that the investor has delivered, both parties usually transact the dollar roll with generic GSE or Ginnie Mae MBS pools that they believe to be of the same or less value than the average TBA-eligible security.

Dollar roll deliveries are made pursuant to TBA Good Delivery Guidelines. Most dollar roll purchase and sale dates conform to the same dates as TBA MBS delivery.[49] The dollar roll market has been noted to have more favorable borrowing rates than the repo market for MBS, which benefits market participants.[50] The dollar roll market also allows dealers and other sellers to acquire pools for delivery to satisfy existing TBA trades, thus avoiding failed trades and providing a tool to manage supply/demand imbalances in the market.[51]

F. Creation and Sales of Private-label MBS

1. Creation of Private-label MBS

A private-label issuer generally creates MBS using whole loans that it either originates or acquires in the secondary whole loan market or uses MBS, including GSE and Ginnie Mae MBS, it acquires in the market. The MBS issuer will assemble pools of mortgage loans that it will deposit into a trust in exchange for MBS. Most private-label MBS are designed to meet specific investor needs; thus, the private label issuer will generally obtain dealer and investor input on the desired characteristics of the various

---

[49] "Consolidating all of an [GSE] agency/coupons trades into a single settlement day each month greatly increases the liquidity of the mortgage market." *Deutsche Bank Report, supra* note 8, at 33.

[50] "A dollar roll transaction transfers prepayment risk to the dealer, who must attach a prepayment assumption to the dollar roll and weigh the risk of forecasting error. Exactly the same par amount of securities is returned in a dollar roll (within TBA variance guidelines). In a repo, the security owner bears the prepayment risk." *Id.* at 32-33.

[51] "Dollar rolls offer dealers a convenient way to obtain promised mortgage securities, avoiding much of the cost of failing to make timely delivery. In theory, the dealer (the short coverer) will be willing to pay up to the cost of failure to deliver for the short-term opportunity to borrow or purchase securities required to meet a delivery commitment. For this reason most dollar rolls are transacted close to the monthly settlement date for mortgage-backed securities. Dollar rolls also allow dealers to even out the supply and demand for mortgage securities in the current settlement month and 'back' months." Biby, Modukuri & Hargrave, *supra* note 37, at 140.

MBS classes to be issued in any particular deal prior to depositing the pool of whole mortgage loans or MBS into the trust. Once the private-label MBS structure is established, the mortgage loans will be deposited into a trust and the MBS sold to investors for cash. The private-label issuer or its affiliates may also retain certain classes of the MBS offered in any deal. Private-label MBS, generally REMICs (backed by both GSE and non-GSE collateral), are composed of specified pools. The diversity of the underlying collateral and credit risk issues heighten investor demand for detailed information to assess prepayment and credit risk.

2. Sales of Private-label MBS

Private-label MBS are not sold in the TBA market. Private-label MBS typically are offered initially through underwriters and generally are not traded on a registered exchange or other organized market. As a result of the fact that private-label MBS have a wide variety of multi-class structures, pool characteristics and issuer standards, they are not fungible and more information about the private-label MBS is provided to facilitate trading. While the private-label MBS market is less liquid than the TBA market, market participants indicate that there is a resale market for many private-label MBS. Because there is no established trading market for resales of private-label MBS, participants in this market must rely on dealer to customer interaction to effect transactions in these securities. The trades are carried out in the over-the-counter market by telephone, fax and e-mail with dealers.

G. Statutes Governing the Offer and Sale of MBS

The GSEs and Ginnie Mae were created by federal legislation, and a number of provisions of federal law exempt their securities from most provisions of the federal securities laws. These exemptions extend to the offer and sale of MBS issued or guaranteed by the GSEs or Ginnie Mae. As discussed below, securities of private-label issuers, including the offer and sale of their MBS, are subject to regulation under these laws.

Ginnie Mae is a wholly-owned corporation of the United States Government under HUD. As such, the securities it guarantees are exempt securities under Section 3(a)(2) of the Securities Act[52] and Section 3(a)(12) of the Exchange Act.[53] The Federal National Mortgage Association Charter Act provides that securities issued or guaranteed by Fannie Mae will be considered exempt securities to the same extent as U.S. Government securities and as such are also exempt in the same manner as securities that Ginnie Mae guarantees.[54] The Federal Home Loan Mortgage Corporation Act contains a similar provision for Freddie Mac.[55] Therefore, GSE and Ginnie Mae MBS may be offered and sold without registration under the Securities Act and the securities are freely

---

[52] 15 U.S.C. § 77c(a)(2).
[53] 15 U.S.C. § 78c(a)(12).
[54] *See* 12 U.S.C. § 1723c.
[55] *See* 12 U.S.C. § 1455g.

tradable securities. Furthermore, the securities are also considered government securities under the Exchange Act and may be traded by government securities brokers.[56] Finally, GSE and Ginnie Mae MBS are also exempt from the Trust Indenture Act of 1939 and the Investment Company Act of 1940.[57]

These exemptions, however, do not mean that the GSEs and issuers of Ginnie Mae MBS are exempt from the antifraud provisions of the federal securities laws. Section 17(a) of the Securities Act, Section 10(b) of the Exchange Act, and Rule 10b-5 promulgated thereunder, apply to all issuers of securities, whether or not the offer and sale is registered under the Securities Act.[58] The antifraud provisions of the federal securities laws prohibit fraudulent or deceptive practices in the offer and sale of MBS. Specifically, the provisions prohibit any person from making a false or misleading statement of material fact. In making disclosures, issuers also may not omit to state a material fact that is necessary in order to make the statements made not misleading. To be considered material, there must be a substantial likelihood that the disclosure of the omitted fact "would have been viewed by the reasonable investor as having significantly altered the 'total mix' of information made available."[59] GSE disclosures are also subject to OFHEO safety and soundness supervision and regulation.

Unlike GSE and Ginnie Mae MBS, offerings of private-label MBS are subject to the registration requirements of the federal securities laws. As such the offer and sale of these securities must be done pursuant to a registration statement filed with the Commission or pursuant to an exemption. The registration statement must meet the Commission's disclosure requirements. If an exemption from the registration requirements is available, the private-label securities may be sold without filing a registration statement with the Commission.[60] Almost all private-label MBS that are not sold pursuant to a registration statement are sold in the 144A market. Rule 144A, a non-exclusive safe harbor from the registration requirements of the Securities Act, permits resales to institutional investors that meet the criteria for "qualified institutional buyer"

---

[56] *See* 15 U.S.C. § 78c(a)(42) - (43). All brokers and dealers in government securities, including banks, must register with or give notice to their appropriate regulatory agency and are subject to certain rules of that agency or their self-regulatory organization, as well as the rules of the Department of the Treasury. *See* 15 U.S.C. § 78o. These rules include certain sales practice provisions, including suitability obligations when making recommendations to certain customers.

[57] *See* 15 U.S.C. § 77aaa – bbbb; 15 U.S.C. § 80a-1 to -64.

[58] *See* 15 U.S.C. § 77q(a); 15 U.S.C.§ 78j(b) and 17 C.F.R. § 240.10b-5. Private-label issuers selling registered MBS are also subject to the liability provisions of Sections 11 and 12 of the Securities Act and Section 18 of the Exchange Act with respect to reports they file with the Commission. *See* 15 U.S.C. § 77k; 15 U.S.C. § 77l and 15 U.S.C. § 78r.

[59] TSC Industries, Inc. v. Northway, Inc., 426 U.S. 438, 449 (1976).

[60] If the private-label securities are sold pursuant to an exemption from registration, the private-label issuer generally would look to a transactional exemption, such as one of the private placement exemptions under Section 4(2), 15 U.S.C. § 77d(2), or Regulation D, 17 C.F.R. § 230.501-.508, promulgated under the Securities Act. Section 4(2) exempts "transactions by an issuer not involving any public offering." Generally the private-label issuer would issue securities under Section 4(2) of the Securities Act in a transaction structured to allow resales pursuant to Rule 144A under the Securities Act.

("QIB") of certain privately placed securities.[61] Rule 144A also contains an information disclosure requirement if the issuer of the securities is not a reporting entity under the Exchange Act.[62] Market participants have indicated that the vast majority of private-label MBS, over 98% in 2001, are sold in registered transactions with the remainder being sold in Rule 144A transactions.[63]

---

[61] *See* 17 C.F.R. § 230.144A. A QIB includes institutional investors that own and invest on a discretionary basis at least $100 million ($10 million for registered securities dealers acting for their own accounts or the accounts of other QIBs) in securities of issuers unaffiliated with the QIBs (with certain limited exclusions). Rule 144A identifies the types of entities that could qualify as QIBs. *See Id.*

[62] For MBS, the servicer or the trustee is considered the issuer of the MBS for purposes of the information requirements of Rule 144A. The Commission stated in the Rule 144A adopting release that, for MBS resales, it would consider information concerning the structure of the securities, distributions on the securities, the underlying assets (type, performance, and servicing information), and credit enhancement mechanism, if any, as satisfying the Rule 144A information requirements. *See* Resale of Restricted Securities, Securities Act Release No. 33-6862 (Apr. 30, 1990). In a 1990 no-action letter, the Commission staff agreed that the issuers could satisfy the information disclosure requirement by contractually requiring the trustee to deliver the required information. Kutak Rock & Campbell, SEC No-Action Letter (Nov. 29, 1990).

[63] *See* Thompson Financial, Mortgage Backed Securities Industry Totals 1996-2001 (Excluding CMBS and Federal Agency Issuances)(Dec. 6, 2002). Various market participants have suggested that disclosure standards in Rule 144A offerings are similar to those in Commission-registered offerings. Given the small percentage of private-label offerings under Rule 144A and the difficulties in accessing documentation of these private transactions, the Task Force did not evaluate disclosure practices in Rule 144A offerings.

III. CURRENT DISCLOSURE PRACTICES

A. General

The content and timing of disclosure vary with the type of issuer and type of security offered. Both private-label and GSE and Ginnie Mae MBS issuers provide disclosure to potential MBS investors in a series of documents and through a variety of means. The MBS structure used, whether pass-through or REMIC, will directly affect the form and content of disclosure, because disclosure will address the terms and risks of the securities being sold. While almost all pass-through MBS are issued by the GSEs or Ginnie Mae issuers, private-label issuers sell primarily REMIC securities. In MBS offerings, disclosure is particularly focused on helping investors evaluate the prepayment and credit risks.

In addition, the different characteristics of the underlying mortgage loans included in GSE and Ginnie Mae MBS and private-label MBS affect the format and content of the disclosures in the respective MBS deals. As discussed above, there have been significant differences, historically, between the mortgage loans underlying GSE and Ginnie Mae MBS and those underlying private-label MBS. Some of these differences between the mortgage loans in GSE and Ginnie Mae or private-label MBS pools may be changing as the GSEs expand their programs to include mortgage loans that may have more or less advantageous payment characteristics than the majority of mortgage loans included in GSE MBS. Because these changes may affect the existing homogeneity of the GSE MBS pools, the changes may also impact the type of information that investors require to assess risk and that the GSEs provide about their MBS pools in the future.

Private-label issuers and the GSEs and Ginnie Mae provide MBS disclosure to investors using different mechanisms. The differences in disclosure delivery arise for two primary reasons. First, while GSE and Ginnie Mae MBS are exempt from the registration and reporting requirements of the federal securities laws, private-label issuers must either file a registration statement meeting the Commission's disclosure requirements or rely on an exemption from registration. Second, GSE and Ginnie Mae pass-through MBS are often sold through a different market, the TBA market, than private-label MBS and GSE and Ginnie Mae REMICs backed by TBA-eligible pass-through MBS. As noted above, the mortgage loans may not even have been made at the time of sale in the TBA market, while the loans have been pooled and described by the time of issuance in the private-label market. Disclosure procedures for providing ongoing information are also different for the GSEs, Ginnie Mae and private-label issuers.

B. Offering Documents

1. Private-label Offering Materials

A private-label issuer that registers the offer and sale of its MBS under the Securities Act must comply with the content and procedural requirements of the

Securities Act covering such offering. In registered offerings under the Securities Act, private-label issuers will disclose material information to investors through the use of two primary documents: the core prospectus and the prospectus supplement. When private-label issuers file a registration statement to register an issuance of MBS, they typically use what is called "shelf registration."[64] Through this process, issuers first file a disclosure document that outlines the parameters of the various types of MBS offerings they may conduct in the future. This document is known as the "core" or "base" prospectus. The registration statement will also contain a form of prospectus supplement, which outlines the format of deal-specific information they will disclose when they later conduct an offering.

In the private-label market, issuers may structure their MBS offerings to meet the particular investment needs of the investors to whom they wish to sell. In this regard, private-label issuers will often provide potential investors with computational materials and structural and collateral term sheets prior to finalizing the deal structure and printing the final prospectus supplement.[65] These materials are intended to help investors understand the proposed transaction and analyze prepayment assumptions and other issues affecting yield. Structural term sheets set out the proposed structure of the securities being offered, such as the parameters of the various types of classes in a REMIC. Private-label issuers using structural term sheets may be required to file them with the Commission and incorporate them by reference into the registration statement for the registered offering.[66] Collateral term sheets provide information regarding the proposed underlying assets. Collateral term sheets, like structural term sheets, may also be required to be filed with the Commission and thereby incorporated by reference into the registration statement. A prospectus supplement describing the terms of the securities the issuer intends to offer, particular risks, information regarding the assets and other deal-specific information may also be prepared and used in the offering process. The final prospectus supplement must be filed with the Commission within two business days following its first use.[67] As noted earlier, if the private-label MBS are not sold pursuant to a registration statement filed with the Commission, the private-label issuer must rely on an exemption from registration to sell the MBS.[68]

---

[64] At the time of enactment of SMMEA, the Commission amended Rule 415, which is known as the shelf rule, to allow SMMEA eligible mortgage related securities to use the shelf offering process. *See* Simplification of Registration Procedures for Primary Securities Offerings, Release No. 33-6964 (Oct. 22, 1992).

[65] *See* Michael S. Gambro & Scott Leichtner, *Selected Legal Issues Affecting Securitization*, 1 N.C. BANKING INST. 131, 146 (Mar. 1997).

[66] *See* Greenwood Trust Company, Discover Card Master Trust I, SEC No-Action Letter (Apr. 5, 1996); Public Securities Ass'n, SEC No-Action Letter (Mar. 9, 1995); Public Securities Ass'n, SEC No-Action Letter (Feb. 17, 1995); Public Securities Ass'n, SEC No-Action Letter, (May 27, 1994); Kidder Peabody, SEC No-Action Letter, (May 20, 1994). Most private-label MBS offerings are registered on Form S-3 for the "shelf", which incorporates by reference into the registration statement future filings by the same issuer. When issuers are required to file structural and collateral term sheets, they file them on Form 8-K, which is then considered to be part of the shelf registration statement.

[67] *See* Instruction 1 to Securities Act Rule 424, 17 C.F.R. § 230.424.

[68] Private-label private placements offering materials generally do not differ widely from those used in registered offerings.

2. GSE and Ginnie Mae Offering Materials

The GSEs and Ginnie Mae are not subject to the registration requirements of the Securities Act in connection with their MBS offerings.[69] The GSEs and Ginnie Mae do not file any MBS offering materials with the Commission. However, the GSEs prepare offering documents similar in form to the core prospectuses filed by private-label issuers in registered offerings and make deal-specific information available through either final prospectus supplements or website disclosures. Fannie Mae and Freddie Mac post their offering documents on their websites. Investors also receive disclosures as part of the settlement process for TBA trades.[70]

Fannie Mae and Freddie Mac provide disclosures to investors through various documents including the base prospectuses and deal specific supplements. Fannie Mae and Freddie Mac also make available information statements that describe their business and operations, as well as include their full audited financial statements. An information statement provides information investors need in order to evaluate the GSEs' guarantees of the MBS. Ginnie Mae, unlike Fannie Mae and Freddie Mac, does not utilize either a core prospectus or prospectus supplement to disclose information regarding its guaranteed pass-through MBS issuances. Instead, Ginnie Mae requires each issuer to use a single required form of disclosure document for the initial MBS sale.

C. Post-Offering Disclosures

1. Private-label MBS

Private-label issuers that have registered the offer and sale of MBS under the Securities Act generally will have a limited mandatory obligation to continue providing information on the MBS.[71] The Exchange Act requires that issuers that have offered and sold securities publicly pursuant to a registration statement must file periodic reports. However, registrants that become subject to reporting requirements pursuant to Section 15(d) of the Exchange Act may discontinue reporting after they file their first annual report on Form 10-K if they have less than 300 record holders.[72] Most MBS issuances

---

[69] *See supra* text accompanying notes 52-57.

[70] Investors receive confirmations of TBA trades. The confirmations will comply with the Good Delivery Guidelines and Rule 10b-10 under the Exchange Act (17 C.F.R. § 240.10b-10) and will provide information regarding the terms of the TBA trade.

[71] *See* 15 U.S.C.§ 78o(d). This assumes that the MBS, as is typically the case, is not trading on an exchange or quoted on an automated quotation system.

[72] *See* 17 C.F.R. § 240.15d-6; 17 C.F.R. § 240.12h-3. MBS issuers, like most fixed-income securities issuers, do not usually register their securities under the Exchange Act and typically have a small number of record holders. Therefore, they are usually able to suspend their reporting obligations on the first day of the fiscal year after their registered offering takes place. In the context of shelf registration statements, where a trust is formed for the issuance of each separate series of securities, a new reporting obligation is incurred by each new trust that is formed and that offers securities under the shelf registration statement. Each trust may stop reporting if it meets the requirements of Section 15(d) of the Exchange Act, notwithstanding the fact that separate trusts of the same sponsor may issue MBS during the fiscal year.

have less than 300 record holders. Therefore, most private-label issuers are not required to continue filing reports with the Commission after they file their first annual report. Although the securities were offered publicly, the small number of investors indicates that the issuer should no longer be considered a public entity. Because of the passive nature of MBS issuers, the staff of the Commission has allowed a modified reporting scheme under the Exchange Act for MBS issuers.[73]

2. GSE and Ginnie Mae MBS

Ginnie Mae and the GSEs provide ongoing disclosure regarding the pools underlying the securities they issue or guarantee.[74] These disclosures generally are provided on a monthly basis for the life of the security through a combination of website disclosures, which vary among the three entities, and disclosures provided by third party information vendors, some of whom purchase information from the GSEs and Ginnie Mae and provide that information to the public for a fee.[75]

D. Particular Issues Addressed by Disclosure

As noted above, the characteristics of the underlying mortgage loans and the marketplace's evaluation of their expected payment speeds will affect the structure,

---

[73] Form 8-Ks are filed based on the frequency of payments on the underlying assets in the trust (but not less than quarterly). These filings include a copy of the servicing or distribution report required by the pooling and servicing agreement or other governing documents regarding the trust. These reports include unaudited information about the performance of the assets, payments on the MBS, and any other material developments that affect the trust.

Private-label issuers also file a modified Form 10-K. This form may aggregate the information in the Form 8-Ks for the fiscal year, respond to other applicable item requirements of the form, and include annual statements from the servicer (or other relevant entity), so long as the private-label issuer continues to be a reporting entity. The servicing information must be reviewed (but not audited) by an independent auditor. Any required exhibits must also be filed. Financial statements are not required. *See, e.g.*, Release No. 34-16520 (Jan. 23, 1980) (order granting application pursuant to Section 12(h) of Home Savings and Loan Association); Release No. 34-14446 (Feb. 6, 1978) (order granting application pursuant to Section 12(h) of Bank of America National Trust and Savings Association); Bay View Securitization Corp., SEC No-Action Letter (Jan. 15, 1998); Key Bank USA, Nat'l Ass'n, SEC No-Action Letter (May 9, 1997); CWMBS, Inc., SEC No-Action Letter (Feb. 3, 1994).

A private-label issuer sometimes continues to provide information to the holders of the MBS after its reporting obligation with the Commission is suspended or even if it was never subject to Exchange Act reporting requirements. This may be because of the terms of the pooling and servicing agreement, the indenture pursuant to which the MBS are issued, the terms of any purchase contract in a Rule 144A or private placement transaction, or the demands of the marketplace. In addition to providing information to the trustee under the indenture, private-label issuers may put MBS performance information on their or the trustees websites or use third party information vendors to disseminate the information.

[74] *See infra* note 79.

[75] For example, with respect to individual pools, Bloomberg LP provides information such as the current weighted average coupon of the pool, the issue and maturity date of the MBS, the weighted average loan age and weighted average remaining maturity as of the most recent factor date, and the original and current unpaid principal balance on the underlying loans. The GSEs have stated that the information that they provide to third party vendors is also either available on their websites or can be calculated from such information.

marketability and risk characteristics of the particular MBS. The yield, or return, on MBS is primarily determined by the timing of payments on the underlying mortgage loans. The underlying mortgage loans in a GSE or Ginnie Mae MBS will often have different payment (including default and prepayment) and other characteristics from those in a private-label MBS. This is due in large part to the eligibility requirements for the underlying mortgage loans and the underwriting standards and guarantee requirements that Ginnie Mae and the GSEs have established for their MBS programs. The effect of these requirements is that the mortgage loans underlying GSE and Ginnie Mae MBS may be less diverse than those underlying private-label MBS. GSE and Ginnie Mae MBS will have more common or homogeneous features and will benefit from the GSE and Ginnie Mae guarantees.

1. Prepayment Risk

As previously discussed, a major risk in an investment in MBS is prepayment risk. Due to the importance of prepayment risk to an investor's decision to invest in MBS, the key disclosures in MBS issuances relate to the various factors that might affect prepayment.

Market participants have developed prepayment models to evaluate prepayment risks. Prepayment models make certain assumptions regarding probable payments on the underlying mortgage loans in order to estimate or predict cash flows.[76] The goal of a prepayment model is to tie together projected mortgage rates and projected prepayment.[77] The more diverse the underlying collateral is in terms of coupons, maturity and loan age, among other characteristics, the greater the need for more detailed information to be able to model for different prepayment scenarios.[78]

2. Credit Risk

As discussed above, credit risk, the risk that the borrowers on the underlying loans may not make timely payments or may default on their loans, is thought by investors to be more significant in private-label MBS than in GSE or Ginnie Mae MBS. Consequently, GSE and Ginnie Mae MBS and the private-label MBS may pose differing degrees of risk for investors. The GSEs and Ginnie Mae guarantee the timely payment of principal and interest on the MBS. The Ginnie Mae guarantee is backed by the full faith and credit of the United States. Fannie Mae and Freddie Mac guarantees do not have United States backing. Investors should look to the audited financial statements and

---

[76] *See* Lowell, *supra* note 10, at 41.
[77] *See* Bykhovsky, *supra* note 25, at 366.
[78] The GSEs may change their underwriting criteria for a variety of reasons. For GSE pools of a given size, expansion of underwriting criteria by the GSEs could lead to decreasing pool homogeneity and increasing unpredictability of pool performance. Changed GSE underwriting criteria would also affect the composition of pools underlying private label MBS and would therefore affect the prepayment behavior of private label securities. *See* Dale Westhoff & V.S. Srinivasan, *The Next Generation of Prepayment Models to Value Nonagency MBS in* THE HANDBOOK OF MORTGAGE-BACKED SECURITIES, *supra* note 10, at 397, 400.

other disclosures of Fannie Mae and Freddie Mac, as well as safety and soundness information provided by OFHEO, to assess the credit risk.

E. Types of Disclosure

Characteristics of the loans backing MBS, of the properties that collateralize the loans, and of the borrowers can have a significant effect on the prepayment and default behavior of the loans and, therefore, on the expected payments to security holders. Market participants have focused on various pieces of information that may help them understand the risk of prepayment or payment failure. Factors that have been most widely noted, including those that are currently disclosed, and some that are not, are discussed below. The GSEs and Ginnie Mae disclosures discussed are only with regard to their pass-through MBS.[79] With respect to Freddie Mac, the discussion below addresses the content and timing of disclosure for its swap program.[80]

1. Loan Terms

The most important loan terms are the interest rates (coupons) paid by the borrowers, the loan maturity dates, the ages of the loans (including origination years), and the sizes of the loans.

a. Coupon or Interest Rates on Underlying Loans

Coupon information is critical because a borrower's financial incentive to prepay a loan depends on the relationship between the coupon and current market rates. The difference between the interest rate on a mortgage loan and the prevailing market interest rate is the most important factor in evaluating the likelihood that the mortgage loan will be prepaid.[81] When interest rates in the market drop and the spread increases between the mortgage loan's interest rate and the available market interest rates, the incentive to refinance an existing loan increases. In order to predict the prepayment of mortgage loans included within a pool underlying MBS, investors look to information that discloses the interest rates of mortgage loans within the MBS pool, and the interest rates that are most prevalent within the pool. One measure of the overall interest rates on

---

[79] While private-label issuers generally provide more information in their Commission filings than the GSEs and Ginnie Mae issuers provide in their offering materials, the information is provided, as to most categories of data, in incremental ranges such as quartiles and not with respect to each mortgage loan within the pool. With respect to the information described in this section and disclosed by the GSEs and Ginnie Mae prior to settlement, that information is generally updated by the GSEs monthly and Ginnie Mae quarterly. As noted in subsequent footnotes, Fannie Mae and Ginnie Mae initially disclose certain items of information after settlement and update the information monthly for Fannie Mae and generally quarterly for Ginnie Mae.

Most pools are composed of fixed-rate loans. For MBS backed by pools of adjustable-rate loans, there is disclosure describing how the future rates are determined.

[80] Freddie Mac's swap program comprises approximately 85% of its fixed rate pass-through MBS issuances. For its cash program, Freddie Mac usually provides similar disclosure, but it is generally provided within two weeks following settlement of the TBA trade.

[81] See LORE & COWAN, *supra* note 7, at 3-3.

mortgage loans underlying a MBS pool is the pool's weighted average coupon, or WAC. The WAC is the average of the coupons on the loans included in the pool, weighted by each loan's outstanding balance.

At issuance, Freddie Mac and private-label issuers typically disclose the WAC for the pool and the distribution of the pool's total unpaid principal balances in various increments across coupon ranges. For example, private label issuers might disclose how much principal of the pool is subject to an interest rate of greater than six percent and less than or equal to 6 1/8 percent.[82] Fannie Mae and Ginnie Mae disclose each pool's WAC prior to settlement.[83]

b. Loan Maturity Dates and Loan Age

Information on original loan maturities (most often 15 or 30 years), remaining maturities, and loan age make it possible for investors to estimate future loan amortization payments. Principal payments increase as loans age, and the payments are lower the longer the original maturities are. The difference between original maturity and remaining maturity may be greater than loan age if borrowers have partially prepaid loans because partial prepayments shorten remaining maturities. Given loan age and original maturity, a shorter remaining maturity implies faster amortization. The longest maturity date of a pool helps investors determine the latest possible date by which scheduled payments on the underlying mortgage loans and, in turn, the MBS should be made.

The weighted average maturity of the pool provides investors with information about the maturity dates of the loans included in the pool. Calculated initially as of the date of pool formation, weighted average maturity is the average of the maturities of the loans included in the pools, weighted by each loan's outstanding balance. Many MBS issuers provide updated maturity information, which is the weighted average remaining maturity of all loans remaining in the pool at the date of calculation. As loans are paid off or prepaid, the number of remaining monthly payments decreases. To the extent prepayments are made, the remaining maturity decreases at a faster rate than it would if borrowers paid only the required amount each month. Thus, investors can evaluate prepayment speeds and make determinations as to when they expect to receive payment on the MBS by examining changes in the pool's weighted average remaining maturity or by comparing the pool's average remaining term to maturity with its weighted average original loan term and weighted average loan age. Unless loan age and loan maturity are evaluated together, prepayments could make a pool look older than it actually is.[84]

---

[82] Freddie Mac discloses information about coupon ranges in the pool by breaking the pool disclosure down into four segments, also known as quartile data.

[83] Fannie Mae discloses WAC quartile data following settlement. Fannie Mae has stated that it will begin disclosing this information prior to settlement in March 2003. Prior to settlement, Fannie Mae discloses the highest and lowest annual interest rates on the underlying mortgage loans. In the Ginnie Mae I program, the coupon rate for all loans is disclosed. In the Ginnie Mae II program, the range, but not the distribution, of loan coupons is disclosed.

[84] *See* WILLIAM W. BARTLETT, THE VALUATION OF MORTGAGE-BACKED SECURITIES 42 (1994).

Information on loan age is also useful in predicting prepayment speeds because prepayments tend to increase during the first few years of newly issued pools and then level out.[85] As a result, most MBS issuers disclose a pool's weighted average loan age or information regarding the prevalence of specific loan origination years within the pool, or both.

Prior to settlement, Freddie Mac discloses each pool's weighted average remaining term to maturity, weighted average loan age, weighted average original loan term, and latest loan maturity date, as well as the total number of loans, unpaid principal balance, and percent of the pool attributed to each loan origination year. Freddie Mac also discloses, again prior to settlement, quartile data for each pool's weighted average maturity, weighted average loan age, and weighted average original loan term. Prior to settlement, Fannie Mae discloses each pool's weighted average remaining term to maturity, latest loan maturity date, number of mortgage loans and unpaid principal balance.[86] Ginnie Mae discloses each pool's weighted average remaining term to maturity, weighted average loan age, and weighted average original loan term prior to settlement.[87] Ginnie Mae also discloses the unpaid principal balance.

Private-label issuers typically provide information similar to that provided by Fannie Mae and Freddie Mac. In their offering documents, most private-label issuers disclose each pool's weighted average remaining term to maturity and some disclose weighted average original loan term. They also sometimes disclose, by ranges of original loan term and either remaining terms to maturity or loan maturity year, the number of loans, aggregate principal balance, and percent of pool principal balance included in each range. Private label issuers also typically disclose either the pool's weighted average loan age, with incremental disclosures comparable to those for remaining term to maturity, or loan origination year.

Finally, MBS issuers generally disclose changes in a pool's aggregate unpaid principal balance. Disclosure of these changes over time may provide useful information regarding the levels of default and prepayment in a particular pool. This is most relevant in a REMIC structure. For example, a larger-than-expected decline in unpaid principal balance may indicate that some of the underlying loans have either defaulted or prepaid at a higher-than-expected rate. MBS issuers generally disclose the aggregate unpaid principal balance of the MBS pool at issuance and update that information monthly. In addition, the GSEs and Ginnie Mae disclose each pool's "current factor" on a monthly basis after settlement. The current factor is a decimal that represents the fraction of the pool's original unpaid principal balance that remains unpaid. The current factor data for

---

[85] *See* LORE & COWAN, *supra* note 7, at 1-6 to 1-7
[86] Fannie Mae discloses weighted average remaining term to maturity, weighted average loan age, and weighted average original loan term quartile data following settlement. Fannie Mae has stated it will begin disclosing this information prior to settlement in March 2003. Fannie Mae also discloses loan origination year information after settlement. It has stated it will disclose weighted average loan age and weighted average original loan term prior to settlement beginning in March 2003.
[87] Following settlement, Ginnie Mae discloses the number of loans in the pool. Ginnie Mae has stated it will disclose the number of loans in the pool prior to settlement beginning in March 2003.

MBS create, over time, a pool history of loan prepayments that is useful in projecting future prepayments.

c. Loan Size

It has been suggested that other than the refinancing incentive, the most important factor in explaining prepayment behavior is loan size.[88] This is because if refinancing costs are fixed, borrowers with larger loan balances will have more incentive to refinance because the costs can be recouped more easily. Also, because loan commissions typically increase with loan size, servicers who solicit borrowers to refinance are more likely to target those with higher principal balances.[89] At issuance, private-label issuers generally provide the average original loan size, together with the number of mortgage loans within a range of balances, the aggregate principal balances of the mortgage loans within each range, and the percentage of the aggregate principal balance of the pool represented by loans in each range. Private-label loan size information is typically presented in increments of $50,000. Prior to settlement, Fannie Mae and Freddie Mac disclose the average original loan size and Freddie Mac discloses quartile data on average original loan size.[90] Prior to settlement, Ginnie Mae discloses only the aggregate original loan balance of the pool, but does not disclose the average original loan size.[91]

d. Points Paid at Settlement

Many borrowers pay points to obtain lower interest rates. The number of points paid, if any, to the lender at the time of loan origination may also be related to likely prepayment behavior. Borrowers who expect to move quickly or are eager to refinance at the earliest opportunity generally seek to avoid points. Also, borrowers with relatively poor credit and higher default risk may be forced to pay points. Prepayment by these borrowers may be less sensitive to interest rate declines but more sensitive to improvements in their credit standing. Neither private-label, the GSEs nor Ginnie Mae MBS issuers typically provide this information. The GSEs do not currently collect such data.

2. Property Information

Property characteristics may also affect expected prepayment and default behavior. The location of the mortgaged properties is of interest to investors, because differences in local or regional economies may affect borrowers. Also, state and local laws may affect the costs of refinancing or the costs of foreclosure.

---

[88] *See* Westhoff & Srinivasan, *supra* note 78, at 410.
[89] *See Id.*
[90] Fannie Mae discloses original loan size quartile data following settlement and has stated it will disclose this information prior to settlement beginning in March 2003.
[91] However, after settlement, Ginnie Mae discloses the number of loans in the pool, so the average original loan size can be calculated after settlement. Ginnie Mae has stated that it will disclose this information prior to settlement beginning in March 2003.

a. Geographic Distribution

Because mortgage loan pools contain a number of mortgage loans, the mortgaged properties securing the mortgage loans in a single pool can be located over a diverse geographic area. Knowing the geographic distributions of the mortgaged properties aids in understanding concentration of credit and prepayment risk. A booming regional housing market, for example, could result in faster prepayment speeds, while a depressed regional job market might increase the credit risk of a pool. To the extent any adverse regional or local economic conditions exist, the smaller the number and the more geographically concentrated the mortgaged properties are, the greater the risk that any regional or localized economic factors will affect payments on the MBS.[92]

Private-label issuers typically disclose in their offering materials the number and aggregate principal balance of mortgage loans secured by properties in each state. They also disclose the percent of the total pool balance represented by loans in each state. Fannie Mae and Freddie Mac also provide this information prior to settlement. Geographic distribution information on mortgaged properties in Ginnie Mae MBS is provided quarterly following the MBS issuance.

b. Property Types

The mortgaged properties can be different property types. Common types include single-family detached, high-rise condos, low-rise condos, two family homes, and three to four family homes. Property type is relevant in analyzing both prepayment and credit risk. Some types of homes, for example single-family detached homes, are often more marketable than others. If a servicer is required to foreclose on a property, there is less risk of loss with a more marketable home. Mortgage loans on single-family homes also default less often than mortgage loans on other types of residential properties.[93]

Private-label issuers typically disclose at issuance the number of mortgage loans and aggregate principal balance outstanding in each property type category, as well as the percent of the pool's aggregate unpaid principal balance within each category. Fannie Mae and Freddie Mac segregate pools based on whether the mortgaged properties are for one to four families or more, but do not provide a breakdown of the type of single family homes. The required Ginnie Mae prospectuses mandate that issuers state whether the underlying mortgage loans are on single or multifamily residences, but no breakdown on type of single-family homes is required.

c. Occupancy Types

The occupancy type of a mortgaged property indicates how the mortgage borrower will use the property. There are generally three types: owner-occupied; second

---

[92] State law can also affect prepayment rates, so it is important to investors to know if the loans are located or concentrated in any state where such laws might affect prepayment.
[93] *See* FRANK J. FABOZZI & DAVID YUEN, MANAGING MBS PORTFOLIOS 134 (1998).

home; and non-owner-occupied properties. Mortgaged properties occupied by the borrower default at a much lower rate than non-owner-occupied properties.[94] Therefore, the occupancy type is relevant to analyzing credit risk of the pool. It is also relevant to prepayment modeling in that, as compared to owner-occupied properties, borrowers on investment properties are more likely to sell the property in an expanding housing market to lock in profits but typically experience more difficulty in refinancing due to greater documentation requirements.[95]

Private-label issuers typically disclose in their offering documents the number of mortgage loans, the aggregate outstanding principal balance, and the percent of the pool's aggregate principal balance for each category of occupancy type. The GSEs do not provide any information with respect to occupancy types of the mortgage loans. All but a de minimis amount of loans in a Ginnie Mae single family pool are owner-occupied.

d. Loan-to-Value Ratio

The loan-to-value ratio of a mortgage loan is a measure of the loan balance compared to the value of the mortgaged property. Typically disclosed as a percentage, LTV is determined by dividing the principal balance of the loan at the date of origination by a measure of the property's value. In the case of a sale, the measure used is the lower of the sale price or the appraised value at the time of sale. In the case of a refinancing, the measure used is the appraised value of the property at the time of the refinancing. In a streamlined refinance underwriting, either the appraised value of the mortgaged property at the time the mortgage being refinanced was originated or an appraised value determined by a limited appraisal report at the time of the refinancing may be used in place of a full appraisal of the mortgaged property.[96]

LTV can be useful in assessing prepayment and credit risk of mortgage loans, and the likely severity of loss in the event of foreclosure.[97] LTV may serve as an indicator of how easily a borrower may be able to refinance or purchase a new home, thus prepaying the outstanding mortgage loan. Loans with higher LTVs are considered more likely to default because the borrower has less invested and has less incentive to retain ownership of the mortgaged property.[98]

Private-label issuers generally disclose in their offering documents the distribution of mortgage loans by original LTV in incremental ranges, for example, five percent increments from 50 percent to 95 percent. For each separate LTV range, private-label issuers generally disclose the number of loans, unpaid balance, and percentage of

---

[94] *See Id.*
[95] *See* Westhoff & Srinivasan, *supra* note 78, at 424.
[96] The appraised value used depends on the LTV percentage at the time of origination of the loan being refinanced.
[97] *See* LORE & COWAN, *supra* note 7, at 1-6.
[98] *See* FABOZZI & YUEN, *supra* note 93, at 87-88.

total pool balance. They also disclose the weighted average original LTV ratio for the pool as a whole. The GSEs and Ginnie Mae do not provide LTV data.

3. Borrower Information

A borrower's financial condition and borrowing purpose can also be indicative of future default and prepayment behavior.

a. Credit Scores

Lenders use a credit score to rank borrowers according to credit risk. One popular type of credit score used is FICO, a credit scoring system developed by Fair Isaac and Company. FICO scores are intended to show the likelihood that an individual might default on a debt based on past credit history. To determine an individual's FICO score, a credit reporting agency using the FICO system will analyze the individual's credit history, including its length, current debt level, payment history, type of credit in use and other new credit inquiries.[99]

Some, but not all, private-label issuers disclose credit scores in varying incremental ranges, such as in 20-point increments. For each credit score range, they may provide the number of mortgage loans, the aggregate unpaid principal balance, and the percentage of total unpaid principal balance. Neither the GSEs nor Ginnie Mae discloses credit scores.

b. Loan Documentation

Mortgage lenders have different levels of documentation that they require prior to making a mortgage loan. The level of documentation required varies with the purpose of the mortgage loan and the credit profile of the borrower. For some borrowers, mortgage lenders may be willing to accept less documentation than they usually require because of the presence of other positive credit factors. Lenders may also agree to originate a loan with less than the full level of documentation they might otherwise require in return for higher origination fees.

Private-label issuers typically provide some loan documentation information. It may be as few as two categories, such as "full documentation" or "reduced documentation," or it may be several different categories depending on what type of documentation levels the lender utilizes. A private-label issuer would typically disclose the number of loans and aggregate outstanding principal balance of mortgage loans underwritten with each level of documentation. The GSEs and Ginnie Mae do not provide such information. The GSEs do not currently collect data on categories of documentation types.

---

[99] *See* FABOZZI & DUNLEVY, *supra* note 21, at 112-13; Fair, Isaac and Company, Inc., *List of FICO Score Factors* (visited Jan. 13, 2003) <http://www.myfico.com/MyFICO/CreditCentral/ScoreConsiders/FICOFactors.asp>.

c. Loan Purpose

There are generally three potential reasons for a borrower to take out a mortgage loan: to purchase a home; to refinance an already-purchased home to obtain a lower interest rate or different payment term; or to refinance a home in order to obtain access to additional funds. The last type is commonly referred to as a cash-out refinance or equity take-out loan. Loans used to purchase homes due to the relocation of a borrower, which are a subset of "purchase" loans, are referred to as relocation loans or relo loans.[100] Investors use information regarding loan purpose to evaluate both credit and prepayment risk. For example, a forecasting model may assume that borrowers whose loan purpose is a cash-out refinance may have more credit risk[101] and are more likely to default[102] than borrowers purchasing a home. Conversely, borrowers who have refinanced in the past may have better credit, be more aware of refinancing opportunities, and, therefore, may be more likely or able to refinance in any future declining interest rate environment.

Private-label issuers generally provide the number of loans in the pool that relate to each of these categories. The information provided also discloses the aggregate outstanding principal balance, and the percent of the pool's aggregate principal balance by each loan purpose type. The GSEs and Ginnie Mae do not provide loan purpose information.

d. Borrower Debt-to-Income Ratios

The ratios of borrowers' required payments on their mortgage debt (or on all of their debt) to their income might provide additional information about their expected default and prepayment behavior. These ratios vary across lenders. While a mortgage loan originator's underwriting standards may have certain debt-to-income caps for mortgage loans, private-label issuers typically do not disclose this information as to the particular mortgage loans in the pool. The GSEs and Ginnie Mae also do not provide debt-to-income information.

4. Sellers, Originators, and Servicers

a. Seller Identification

The seller of a loan is the entity that sells the mortgage loan to the MBS issuer. The originator is the lender that made the mortgage loan to the borrower. Originators often sell the loans they originate directly to MBS issuers in order to obtain ready access

---

[100] *See* FABOZZI & YUEN, *supra* note 93, at 19.
[101] *See* Westhoff & Srinivasan, *supra* note 78, at 425; Thomas Zimmerman & Kumar Neelakantan, *Credit Performance of High LTV Loans in* THE HANDBOOK OF MORTGAGE-BACKED SECURITIES, *supra* note 10, at 329, 339.
[102] *See* Zimmerman & Neelakantan, *supra* note 101, at 339 (noting that cash-out refinancings reduce the equity a borrower has in the home).

to additional lending capital. Because of this, the seller and the originator are in most cases the same entity. However, since whole loans may be bought and sold in the secondary market, it is possible for an entity to sell to an MBS issuer whole loans that it did not originate, in which case the seller and the originator are different. Moreover, sellers or originators may sell servicing rights. The identity of the originator of a loan could be relevant for both credit and prepayment risk. With regard to credit risk, it is important to identify those originators that have less stringent underwriting standards because they are likely to include loans with greater credit risk in MBS pools. Identity of the seller could also be relevant to prepayment to the extent the seller originates loans primarily in areas where there is greater prepayment of mortgage loans.

In private-label offerings the seller's name is disclosed in the prospectus supplement. Private-label issuers also sometimes disclose the amount of the pool, by number of loans or unpaid principal balance, which other lenders originated. Freddie Mac discloses the name of the seller prior to settlement and Fannie Mae discloses the name of the seller after settlement.[103] For Ginnie Mae's single-seller pools, the seller is disclosed prior to settlement. For its multiple issuer pools, the sellers are identified post-settlement.

b. Servicer Identification

The servicer is the entity that collects payment of the underlying loans and distributes payments on the MBS to the MBS holders either directly or through a trustee. The servicer collects a fee for performing these responsibilities as set forth in a servicing agreement with the issuer of the MBS. Servicer identification may allow investors to make assumptions regarding the expected prepayment risk. Servicers can be either master servicers or subservicers.[104] Mortgage research analysts currently compile reports ranking the prepayment speeds of mortgage loans serviced by different servicers.[105] Some servicers are also originators and they may try to solicit the borrowers into refinancing. In addition, pools may include loans that have different servicers or that have master servicers.

Some private-label issuers may identify only master servicers in their offering documents, while others identify subservicers as well. Neither Fannie Mae nor Freddie Mac discloses the identity of servicers. In the Ginnie Mae I program the servicer is disclosed prior to settlement and in the Ginnie Mae II program the servicers are disclosed following settlement.

---

[103] Freddie Mac does not disclose the name of the seller for MBS issued under its cash program, where the pools include multiple sellers. Fannie Mae has stated it will disclose the name of the seller prior to settlement beginning in March 2003.

[104] Master servicers enter into the servicing agreement with the MBS issuer and are usually permitted to delegate some of their servicing responsibilities to other servicers.

[105] *See, e.g.*, J.P. Morgan Securities, Inc., *Mortgage Research, Mortgage Servicers Prepayment Report* (Apr. 8, 2002). Because the terms servicer and seller are frequently used interchangeably, it is not always clear as to which entity the information relates.

IV. INFORMATION IMBALANCE ISSUES

Some market participants have expressed concern that participants in the MBS markets use information they obtain in their capacities as originators, guarantors and servicers, among others, to select for purchase, sale or retention MBS or underlying mortgage loans that have more favorable characteristics than the average universe of MBS or mortgage loans. Assertions have been made that these entities have an unfair advantage over the marketplace generally in purchasing and selling MBS. In order to evaluate these concerns, it is important to note that at each level of the process of creating and selling MBS, the market participants involved will make certain choices about which mortgage loans or MBS to retain or sell. For example, lenders or pool sponsors select the underlying mortgage loans that they will securitize. Investors may also decide, at the time of a trade that they wish to purchase MBS having certain characteristics.

To review concerns about "favorable selection" or "cherry picking" based on possible information imbalances, it is also important to understand that market participants might view a transaction differently. In order to understand how selection practices may raise issues in the markets, it is helpful to identify the situations that raise a concern for some market participants.

First, some market participants are concerned that when other market participants routinely decide to keep purchased or created MBS in their portfolio, they are relying on information not generally available in making these decisions. In the MBS market, situations exist where a market participant may determine to buy, sell or hold a security or mortgage loan in its portfolio based on information in its possession and not otherwise publicly available. Entities have different reasons for determining to buy, sell or retain securities or mortgage loans, including their knowledge of the product and their business goals and objectives. Any entity involved in originating a mortgage, compiling a pool of mortgages for securitization or creating a MBS may have detailed information about the characteristics of the underlying mortgage loans. Determinations about what securities to keep or sell remain within the control of the originator, sponsor or holder of the MBS.

The Task Force understands that information is not provided for various reasons, including the fact that specific information is not generated or available to the MBS seller, there has been a lack of market demand for particular information, or disclosing the information could cause competitive harm. MBS issuers and originators might not reveal all the information in their possession about the MBS. Some market participants have indicated that even if the information is revealed to the initial purchaser, such information may not be disclosed to the marketplace generally.

A second concern expressed was that, in addition to having business reasons to keep MBS in their portfolios, market participants use information that is not generally available to make portfolio decisions. Once the MBS is originated, securitized or purchased, the originator, securitizer or purchaser may determine to keep the highest quality of the MBS in its portfolio. The decision to keep MBS or mortgage loans in a portfolio also may be made about lesser quality products where a market may not exist or may not provide a fair price for a lower quality asset.

Purchasing, originating or securitizing MBS or a mortgage loan and keeping it in a portfolio may be desirable for a number of reasons, such as investment and other business reasons. This practice has been termed "culling." It should be noted that market participants are under no obligation to distribute MBS or mortgage loans with any particular characteristics and that purchasers establish MBS prices according to their analysis of the relative value of the assets and the securities being offered.[106] As with any other industry, MBS market participants are entitled to manage their own assets and portfolios.

Finally, the Task Force heard that a central concern for market participants was that an originator or guarantor of MBS might purchase MBS in secondary trades through their investment arm based on information about particular securities not generally disclosed or available to the public, giving the internal or affiliated investment department the ability to use such information to the detriment of other prospective purchasers or sellers. Here the concern is that MBS sold into the market with information is purchased back at some later time based on information greater than that held by the current seller. The antifraud provisions of the federal securities laws prohibit persons from making fraudulent misuse of material inside information in connection with the offer and sale of securities.[107] Bank regulatory and OFHEO rules also address this issue.[108]

Market participants generally have in place policies and procedures to assure compliance with legal requirements. The Task Force confirmed, for example, that Fannie Mae and Freddie Mac have written policies to address internal sharing of information. These policies include their codes of conduct that prohibit insider trading and their internal safeguards (termed "firewalls" or "information barriers") that prevent information sharing among divisions, primarily loan level data acquired as part of the guarantor function for securitization that cannot be shared with the investment function that seeks to purchase MBS for portfolio. The goal of these policies is to prevent the trading desks at Fannie Mae and Freddie Mac from receiving information that is available only to Fannie Mae and Freddie Mac as a result of their purchases of underlying mortgage loans or in their capacities as guarantors. Under the policies, the trading desks should trade with the same information available to other market purchasers. The

---

[106] Further, regulated firms such as banks, thrifts and GSEs have legislative and regulatory incentives to maintain assets that are of a high quality.
[107] *See* 17 C.F.R. § 240.10b-5, 10b5-1 to 10b5-2.
[108] *See e.g.*, BOARD OF GOVERNORS OF THE FEDERAL RESERVE SYSTEM, TRADING AND CAPITAL MARKETS ACTIVITIES MANUAL §2150.1, at 212 (1998) (discussing conflicts of interest issues). For OFHEO rules and guidance *see* 12 C.F.R. § 1710.1-.20 (corporate governance rule; systems of internal control and conflict of interest standards) and 12 C.F.R. § 1720 apps. A (internal controls and information technology) & C (policy guidance-- safety and soundness standards for information). *See also* OFFICE OF FEDERAL HOUSING ENTERPRISE OVERSIGHT, EXAMINATION HANDBOOK at ch. 2 (1998)(internal controls and separation of duties and responsibilities).

allegation was made that the GSEs' own mortgage asset portfolios performed better than the outstanding MBS guaranteed by the GSEs. The Task Force found this in itself to be unpersuasive as the GSEs' mortgage portfolios include other instruments and the GSEs, like other investors, may hold better portfolios by purchasing better performing MBS that they select on the basis of publicly available information for which they may pay a higher price. No evidence was brought forward of any impropriety in creating their portfolio mix.

As part of its continuous examination of Fannie Mae and Freddie Mac, OFHEO reviews each GSE's internal controls and corporate policies, including their firewall policies, and examines each GSE to ascertain its financial safety and soundness, including compliance with internal controls and policies. OFHEO reports annually to Congress on its examination findings and on any enforcement actions that OFHEO has undertaken that year. An OFHEO review of GSE practices and data on portfolio prepayment performance did not support a conclusion that "cherry picking" occurred.[109] In interviews in connection with preparing this report, no market participant presented substantiated evidence to the contrary. As primary regulator of the GSEs, OFHEO will continue to closely monitor GSE compliance in this area.

---

[109] It should be noted that slower prepayment speeds are not necessarily indicative of "cherry picking."

V. FINDINGS

The Task Force made the following findings based on its review of current disclosures in the mortgage-backed securities markets and its consideration of enhancements to such disclosure.

1. <u>Additional Pool Level Disclosures Are Justified and Expected to have Minimal Disruption on the Functioning of the MBS Markets</u>

The purpose of this study was to examine the current state of disclosure in the markets for MBS with a view to determining whether enhancements in disclosure practices would be useful. The Task Force finds that, given the current state of the MBS market, enhanced disclosure by MBS issuers – particularly by the GSEs that issue securities in these markets – would be both justified and feasible on a pool (aggregate) basis.

Disclosing a broader amount of information could assist investors in their decision-making, improve efficiency, pricing, and market confidence, and, insofar as it improves market quality and transparency, enhance safety and soundness. The Task Force believes that carefully selected and implemented enhancements can also be made without disruption to the functioning of the current market, particularly the TBA market, or unreasonable cost to market participants. Collectively, the U.S. MBS markets are the predominant sector of U.S. fixed-income markets. In general, the Task Force finds the MBS markets for GSE and Ginnie Mae MBS to be robust, flexible, efficient and liquid. The TBA market, which is the forward commitment market for pass-through MBS, is the largest, most liquid, and perhaps most important of these markets. Because the TBA market consists entirely of GSE and Ginnie Mae MBS, the Task Force has focused its attention on this market.

Market participants agree that the TBA market is vital to the efficiency, flexibility, and liquidity of the GSE and Ginnie Mae MBS market, which are the largest component of, and the benchmark for, the MBS markets. As the TBA market has evolved, the GSEs have progressively expanded their disclosures with little adverse impact on the market. In fact, these additional disclosures have enhanced market transparency, confidence, stability, and discipline. Although the GSEs have indicated that they regard the current level of disclosure as adequate, many large and smaller market participants indicated that they would find timely disclosure of additional information useful, primarily for enhanced prepayment risk analysis. As discussed below, prepayment risk analysis has become more sophisticated in recent years. Some market participants perceive issues of information asymmetry given these changes in prepayment risk analysis and other developments in the MBS market in recent years, including mortgage industry consolidation, a marginally less homogenous TBA market due to increased volumes of stipulated trades, and the growth in GSEs' retained portfolios.

During the study, the GSEs and some market participants maintained that additional disclosure could adversely affect liquidity or efficiency in the TBA market by fragmenting the market. However, even the GSEs acknowledge that the TBA market is more liquid than ever before, while it is less homogenous and more fragmented than it was five or six years ago due, in part, to increasing sophistication of borrowers and investors, greater refinements to prepayment models, and, as a result, more stipulated trades. The first step in the current pooling process can, therefore, involve screening loans for characteristics, including those related to prepayment risk, that may command a premium on the TBA market.

The Task Force finds more persuasive the arguments of other investors and market participants who counter that any adverse effects from additional disclosure would be short-term, and ultimately would be outweighed by the benefits of greater information flowing into, and therefore more informed analysis of, the MBS market. For example, enhanced disclosure could better enable investors to analyze and predict prepayments and other risks, which may help them to make more informed investment decisions. While this might lead to some further fragmentation, it should also eventually result in more efficient pricing of mortgage products available to individual borrowers. TBA pricing is the basis for pricing for other segments of the MBS market, and, therefore, improvements in TBA pricing could extend to the pricing of other MBS products.

2. Implementation of Additional Disclosures Through Market Action

The market participants the Task Force interviewed identified a large number of possible disclosure items. Of the possible additional disclosure items identified in the interviews, this report highlights those disclosure items that a significant number of participants said may have predictive value in analyzing prepayments. Within this group of highlighted disclosure items, the Task Force also considered whether the information is reasonably available. The Task Force believes investor interest and issues of practicality should be important determinative criteria as to whether and under what circumstances particular disclosure items would add value and market participants and the market would best make these determinations.

The Task Force believes that additional elements of disclosure in the MBS market could be determined and implemented, as it has in the past, through guidelines agreed upon by market participants, including large and small investors, broker-dealers, industry groups and other market participants. Such determinations could include the appropriate timing and method of providing additional disclosure. As a supplement to this process, the GSEs could create greater homogeneity by revising their underwriting guidelines or pooling requirements. If market forces are unable to reach consensus on disclosure enhancements, the agencies represented on the Task Force will need to consider what additional action might be appropriate.

3. Potential Items Suggested for Enhanced Disclosures in the MBS Markets

During Task Force interviews with various market participants a number of items were repeatedly mentioned as candidates for enhanced disclosure especially with regard to TBA-eligible securities. The Task Force found that market participants generally sought aggregate pool information - as opposed to loan-level information - perhaps expressed in quartiles or other standardized breakdowns. Based on current mortgage underwriting and purchase practices - automated and otherwise - disclosure of certain of these items may be more readily achieved than others.

Market participants suggested that the following additional pool-specific information would present few practical obstacles:

- loan purpose (*i.e.,* whether a purchase or refinance)
- original loan-to-value (LTV) ratios
- standardized credit scores of borrowers
- servicer for the pool (this may not always be the seller or originator)
- occupancy status (owner-occupied or investor)
- property type (*e.g.,* detached, condo)

The Task Force believes that these additional disclosures could benefit the MBS markets and urges market participants to give serious consideration to implementing these disclosures.

The above information is generally collected by loan originators and, to the extent it is not already, could be provided to whole-loan mortgage purchasers (*i.e.,* MBS issuers), and passed on in appropriate form to market participants. For example, GSEs do not receive standardized credit scores from sellers for all mortgage loans, but the information is not difficult for the GSE issuer to obtain. Although the items listed above may not present practical difficulties, they may entail data quality issues. For example, it was noted that the timing of a credit rating might affect the borrower's score. Similarly, the quality of LTV data may be affected if, for example, originators do not use updated appraisal information in calculating the LTVs for mortgage loans.

In addition to the list of items set forth above, a number of other possible desirable disclosure enhancements were mentioned in interviews with market participants. Although the consensus is less clear with respect to these items, the Task Force believes they should be given consideration as subjects of enhanced disclosure. Other requested information included debt-to-income ratio, points paid, and level of documentation (*e.g.,* high, medium, low). The Task Force heard from some market participants about possible drawbacks to collecting and disclosing this information. For example, Fannie Mae and Freddie Mac generally do not collect information on points from loan originators. With respect to documentation, because different lenders employ different standards (*e.g.,* "low doc" may mean different levels of documentation to different lenders), industry-wide standards or common nomenclature would need to be devised and implemented. Finally, although debt-to-income is often available from lenders, it is subject to the varying standards originators use to verify the borrowers assets and liabilities.

4. <u>The Task Force Did Not Receive Substantiation of Allegations of Improper Activity Based on Information Imbalances</u>

Apart from issues of disclosure, the Task Force also heard allegations of selective selling and purchasing practices tied to possible information imbalances, so-called "cherry picking." The allegations included claims that Fannie Mae and Freddie Mac have made improper use of non-public information for trading purposes. No evidence was brought forward to the Task Force, including by those making allegations, that would have substantiated these claims. Moreover, the GSEs maintain policies intended to prevent improper information sharing. Further, slower prepayment speeds in retained portfolios of the GSEs is not totally unexpected because the GSEs, like private issuers and loan originators, may sell or purchase MBS with a goal of creating and maintaining their own strong portfolios.

5. <u>Ginnie Mae Enhancements to MBS Market Disclosures</u>

Ginnie Mae indicated to the Task Force that, as a matter of policy, it believes that full and accurate disclosure on all aspects of its MBS and underlying collateral is important. Ginnie Mae has developed, and continues to refine, procedures for monitoring and disseminating information relating to its MBS.

Ginnie Mae is currently in the process of evaluating the enhancement of disclosure of information on its securities. In particular, Ginnie Mae has been asked by market participants to provide credit information, such as credit scores and loan-to-value ratio information. Ginnie Mae is reviewing these requests in light of information available to it and its ability to obtain accurate information. Ginnie Mae has advised the Task Force that certain items of requested information are not required to be provided under the FHA, VA or other relevant underwriting guidelines for Ginnie Mae eligible mortgage loans.

6. <u>Regulatory Oversight</u>

The Treasury, OFHEO and the Commission expect to monitor the MBS markets in general, and the TBA market in particular, to evaluate the implementation and impact of disclosure enhancements, in assisting investors in evaluating securities in the MBS markets and making informed investment decisions. If future developments warrant, the Task Force members, in their separate capacities or jointly as they agree appropriate, could consider what additional steps may further enhance disclosures to investors in the MBS marketplace.

In addition, with regard to non-exempt securities offerings, including MBS, the Commission is continuing to study the need for a comprehensive regulatory framework for all registered asset-backed securities offerings. OFHEO is continuing its oversight and examination of the GSEs' operations and practices in their role as the GSEs' safety and soundness regulator.

APPENDIX A

Meetings and Interviews

The Task Force interviewed the following firms, groups and individuals:

The Bond Market Association
Alan Boyce, Portfolio Manager, Soros Fund Management
California State Teacher's Retirement System (CALSTRS)
Countrywide Home Loans, Inc. and Countrywide Securities Corporation
Fannie Mae
FM Watch
Freddie Mac
Ginnie Mae
Dr. Dwight Jaffee (Haas School of Business, University of California, Berkeley)
Mortgage Bankers Association of America
Scott Simon of PIMCO
Phillip Thigpen, Jr. (Phillip Thigpen, Jr., a financial advisory firm)
Peter Wallison (American Enterprise Institute)
Washington Mutual Bank, FA, Washington Mutual Mortgage Securities Corp., and Long Beach Mortgage Company

APPENDIX B

Summary of Part III.E., "Types of Disclosure"

These tables summarize the information in Part III.E., "Types of Disclosure." The tables compare the content of disclosures provided by Ginnie Mae and the GSEs with respect to their pass-through MBS offerings and private-label issuers, generally, with respect to their REMIC offerings, in each case, except as otherwise noted, at or prior to settlement.[1] The tables do not address differences in the timing of pre-settlement disclosure or amount or frequency of any ongoing disclosure. Reference should be made to the detailed discussion in Part III.E.

Loan Terms	Fannie Mae	Freddie Mac[2]	Ginnie Mae	Private Label[1]
Disclosure Item		(Pass-through MBS)		(REMICs)
Weighted average coupon	Yes	Yes	Yes	Yes
Distribution of loan coupons within pool	Yes, post-settlement[3,4]	Yes	Variable[5]	Yes
Weighted average remaining term to maturity	Yes	Yes	Yes	Yes
Distribution of remaining terms to maturity or loan maturity year within pool	Yes, post-settlement[4]	Yes	No	Variable
Weighted average loan age	Yes, post-settlement[4]	Yes	Yes	Yes
Distribution of loan ages or loan origination years within pool	Yes, post-settlement[4]	Yes	No	Variable
Weighted average original loan term	Yes, post-settlement[4]	Yes	Yes	Variable
Distribution of original loan terms within pool	Yes, post-settlement[4]	Yes	No	Variable
Latest maturity date of loans in pool	Yes	Yes	No	Yes
Number of loans in pool	Yes	Yes	Yes, post-settlement[6]	Yes
Unpaid principal balance	Yes	Yes	Yes	Yes
Average original loan size	Yes	Yes	Yes, post-settlement[6]	Yes
Distribution of original loan sizes within pool	Yes, post-settlement[4]	Yes	No	Yes
Points paid	No	No	No	No

Property Information	Fannie Mae	Freddie Mac[2]	Ginnie Mae	Private Label[1]
Disclosure Item		(Pass-through MBS)		(REMICs)
Distribution of mortgaged properties' geographic locations	Yes	Yes	Yes, post-settlement	Yes
Distribution of property types within pool (e.g., single-family detached, high rise condo, low rise condo)	No	No	No	Yes
Distribution of occupancy types within pool (e.g., owner-occupied, second home, non-owner-occupied)	No	No	Yes[7]	Yes
Weighted average original loan to value ratio	No	No	No	Yes
Distribution of original loan to value ratios within pool	No	No	No	Yes

Borrower Information	Fannie Mae	Freddie Mac[2]	Ginnie Mae	Private Label[1]
Disclosure Item		(Pass-through MBS)		(REMICs)
Distribution of credit scores within pool	No	No	No	Variable
Distribution of loan documentation information (e.g., full, reduced, streamlined)	No	No	No	Yes
Distribution of loan purpose within pool (e.g., purchase, rate/term refinance, cash-out refinance)	No	No	No	Yes
Debt to income ratios of borrowers	No	No	No	No

Seller, Originator and Servicer Information	Fannie Mae	Freddie Mac[2]	Ginnie Mae	Private Label[1]
Disclosure Item		(Pass-through MBS)		(REMICs)
Seller identity	Yes, post-settlement[4]	Yes[8]	Variable[9]	Yes
Portion of pool originated by others than seller	No	No	No	Variable
Servicer information	No	No	Yes	Yes

---

[1] Because of the relatively diverse group of issuers in the private-label market, there is substantial but not complete uniformity to the information disclosed in the offering materials of SEC-registered private-label MBS. As to private-label issuers, therefore, the chart indicates the typical or normal practice with respect to disclosure, as discussed further in the text. As a result, where it is indicated in the charts that disclosure is provided there are almost certainly cases where such disclosure is not provided. Conversely, where it is indicated that disclosure is not provided, there may well be cases where such disclosure is provided. Where the chart indicates that practice is variable for private-label issuers, the Task Force has been unable to identify a significantly predominant pattern of disclosure for the category.

[2] The discussion in Part III.E. of the report addresses the content and timing of disclosure for Freddie Mac's swap program. Freddie Mac's swap program comprises approximately 85% of its fixed-rate pass-through MBS issuances. For its cash program, Freddie Mac usually provides similar disclosure, but it is generally provided within two weeks following settlement of the TBA trade.

[3] Prior to settlement, Fannie Mae discloses the highest and lowest annual interest rates on the loans in the pool.

[4] Fannie Mae has stated it will begin disclosing this information prior to settlement in March 2003.

[5] In the Ginnie Mae I program the coupon rate for all loans is disclosed. In the Ginnie Mae II program, the range, but not the distribution, of loan coupons is disclosed.

[6] Ginnie Mae has stated it will disclose the number of loans in the pool prior to settlement beginning in March 2003. At that time it will be possible to determine the average original loan size prior to settlement.

[7] All but a de minimis amount of loans in a Ginnie Mae single-family pool are owner-occupied.

[8] Freddie Mac discloses the seller in its swap program but not in its cash program, where the pools include multiple sellers.

[9] For Ginnie Mae's single-seller pools, the seller is disclosed prior to settlement. For its multiple-issuer pools, the sellers are identified post-settlement.

www.ingramcontent.com/pod-product-compliance
Lightning Source LLC
Chambersburg PA
CBHW081904170526
45167CB00007B/3142